D0775156

THE D.R.E. BOOK

THE D.R.E. BOOK

*Questions and Strategies
for Parish Personnel*

by
Maria Harris

PAULIST PRESS
New York/Paramus/Toronto

BV
1531
.H33

Copyright © 1976 by
The Missionary Society
of St. Paul the Apostle
in the State of New York

All rights reserved. No part of this book may be reproduced or transmitted in
any form or by any means, electronic or mechanical, including photocopying,
recording or by any information storage and retrieval system, without permis-
sion in writing from the Publisher.

Library of Congress
Catalog Card Number: 75-44803

ISBN: 0-8091-1938-2

Published by Paulist Press
Editorial Office: 1865 Broadway, N.Y., N.Y. 10023
Business Office: 400 Sette Drive, Paramus, N.J. 07652

Printed and bound in the
United States of America

Contents

CONCORDIA COLLEGE LIBRAR
2811 N. E. HOLMAN ST.
PORTLAND, OREGON 97211

v

CONCORDIA COLLEGE LIBRARY

To
Rev. Frederick F. Schaefer
with gratitude and affection

1
Introduction

No question is more unnerving to the Parish Coordinator than the innocently-phrased, "But what do you DO all day?" On the one hand, the question may jar already-frayed nerves because the one constant in the life of ninety percent of practicing DRE's is they do too much.[1] On the other, the question is usually put directly and simply because many people in the churches are genuinely unaware not only of what a Coordinator does, but, more basically, of what a Coordinator is. The phenomenon of the Coordinator is so new in Roman Catholicism and the activities of the Coordinator so varied that even the persons responsible for hiring Coordinators are often hard put to answer the question accurately and directly. The phenomenon tends to be more stereotyped in Protestantism, but the role is still unknown to many.

The phenomenon of the Coordinator as it exists today *is* new, although in the United States, at least since the turn of the century, several religious orders have existed whose main work was "catechetical," while in Protestantism the DRE or Minister of Christian Education has been on the scene for many years. The most startling dimensions of the role as it has grown in the past decade are the large number of people who have chosen this as their work, and the fact that the role is an evolving one, a work-in-process. No one seems quite sure exactly what is involved as yet, and many Coordinators find that after their first

---

1. The phrases "Parish Coordinator" and "DRE" will be used interchangeably throughout this book, as they are in actual practice, with the latter more often heard in Protestantism and the former in Catholicism. Necessary distinctions will be made as they are needed.

year in a given parish an entirely new job description must be worked out. It is with an understandable degree of tentativeness, therefore, that the following pages are presented.

At this time, the role has evolved to that of a person who is a hired, salaried professional engaged by a parish to direct, organize and/or consolidate religious education programs within the parish. Obviously, the closing of parochial schools has been a major factor in the growth of the Coordinator's position, but it would be both superficial and naive to cite this as the only one. A renewed emphasis on adulthood, the communications explosion, and the collapse of traditional institutions in our contemporary world are influences at least as strong.

This point is one that cannot be made too strongly. To see the kind of role a Coordinator plays as a phenomenon exclusive to the Catholic Church is to look with the ghettoized and myopic viewpoint that considers the world of the last part of the twentieth century an ecclesiocentric one. A more realistic assessment of the situation would include an acknowledgment that the Coordinator is not just a new role within the church, created in response to an ongoing crisis. The Coordinator is a new *kind* of role in a church that is already a radically different kind of religious institution because of that church's existence in a radically different, post-bureaucratic, technological world. The Coordinator is a new kind of co-official in the church, non-ordained yet fulfilling many roles formerly assigned to the ordained. In part, this is because the modern communitarian emphasis demands another way of exercising authority and leadership. Equally, if not more important in today's world, there is a call for a mutual interchange of authority and power not just among men, but among women, and between women and men as well. To all of these cultural currents, the Coordinator is a testament.

Tied to this new kind of role is a vision of its future. Many Coordinators will comment, after a year or two in a parish, that their desire is to "put themselves out of a job." This may be understood in several different ways. One is that the Coordinator is someone who is doing a work within the religious community that can and ought to be done by anyone and everyone else. The really good, really professional DRE does her or his work best when the rest of the church membership begins to do it too. Ministering, teaching, and being available for listening are activities not confined to a job. Another implication is paradoxical. That is, a Coordinator is someone who does a very specific kind of work. No one else can do or is doing it; it is the reason a Coordinator is hired. She or he has a professional set of skills requisite to the task, which other community members do not possess—for example, training in theology, education, and, more recently, administration.

Both of these implications are accepted in this book. It is one of its theses that they go together. Most of the book will concentrate on the second: the specific things a DRE, and, by extension, other parish personnel, do. But the fabric of the Coordinator's doing is the fact that it is set within the context of the first. The Coordinator does what everyone else in the church is called to do, and when he or she is really good at it, everyone else in the church begins doing, and being, the same thing as the Coordinator.

What then does a Coordinator do? Some time ago, Stephen Nevin, then Diocesan Director of Religious Education in Ogdensburg, New York, devised the helpful Anstep formula, which carefully focused on three major areas of concern to DRE's. Nevin wrote[2] that the Coordinator was (a) a theological resource person; (b) a master teacher; (c) an organizer or manager. He suggested that in deciding on a job, an individual would do well to weigh personal competence and interest in these three areas and ideally match them against a particular parish's expectations in the same three areas.[3] The point I wish

2. Stephen Nevin, "Parish Coordinator: Evaluating Task and Roles," *The Living Light*, Vol. 9, #1, Spring 1972, pp. 48-56.
3. On a scale to equal no more than 15, one could thus rate talent and/or preference as well as expectation as 9-3-3 for someone strong in theology but weaker in education and administration, or 0-6-9 for a parish desiring an organizational person with a strong education background. The point is to match person and parish as well as possible.

to emphasize here is the selection of the three areas. I agree with Nevin that they are the critical ones: administration, religious or theological reflection, education. But I would add that they are the concerns of everyone today called to participate in parish and other religious communities. All are called to the sharing of power and authority as members of the organism (or organization) of the church. Each member is a religious person, sharing a religious life, which is to say that there is a religious dimension to each one's experience, and that the terms "religious woman" and "religious man" have currency only as a description of each man and woman. Finally, education broadly conceived in the Deweyan tradition as the reconstruction of experience and the reflection upon that experience is the concern not just of someone called a Coordinator—who may be a master teacher—but of everyone in the community.

Within this wide framework, where the church of today lives its life, the microcosm of the parish exists. And it is within the parish that we find individual Coordinators today. How best describe what they do? Is that at all possible?

Because of the ambiguity of the terms parish and coordinator, both of which will be dealt with in subsequent chapters, a job description for the Coordinator can only be sketched in general terms. Parishes, by their nature, differ in size, geography, socio-economic levels, personnel and pastoral emphases. Coordinator can and does subsume within itself such meanings as director, organizer, planner, administrator, teacher and resource person, as well as many other activities related to these broader areas. In general, however, it is true that the work of the Coordinator presently falls into three general areas, already alluded to in commenting on the Anstep formula. One of these may take more of the Coordinator's time and be her or his focus of concern more than the others. This is particularly dependent on other personnel available, factors specific to an individual parish, and differing interests and needs of people within the parish community, as well as the particular talents of the DRE. Nevertheless, the three areas are administration, education and religion.

Administration includes many duties: planning, implementing, scheduling, securing faculty for, and supervising programs for senior citizens, adults, parents, young adults of college age, high school students, junior high students, elementary school children, pre-schoolers, family programs, and programs in preparation for the reception of the sacraments. This last includes all of the sacraments, with the possible exception of holy orders, although, with the renewed emphasis on ministry, that too appears to be changing. Administration also involves the necessary office routine attached to such work, and many Coordinators find their work rendered ineffective through a lack of secretarial assistance. Lastly, the connections between administration and ministry are semantically and actually of major importance.

Education includes such tasks as the selection and distribution of curriculum materials, the formation of and actual instruction in programs where teachers are trained in pedagogy, the design of suitable educational environments for particular programs, the screening, choice and purchase of library and audio-visual equipment, hardware and software, and the supervision and observation of faculty in actual teaching situations, with the meetings, conferences and evaluative reflection involved in such activities. Perhaps master teacher or educational resource person is more accurate terminology, but the point is that the DRE is a catalyst for much of what occurs educationally, both formally and informally, in the parish.

In the area of religion, the religious and theological resources of the Coordinator are called on in the development and execution of programs, as well as in the choice of materials appropriate to various ages and backgrounds. This aspect of the task carries with it the necessity for a continued and educated awareness of religious and theological trends with the reading and professional conference-attendance often entailed. On a more personal level, the Coordinator's role may take the form of sister or brother confessor within the community, where he or she is called on to act as counselor, guide and friend. Of great importance, too, is the DRE's ability to reflect theologically with other community members on their life and action together.

Other important tasks in which the Coordinator is often engaged include: communication through mailings, monthly newsletters, memos; attendance at innumerable parish and neighborhood meetings (most DRE's average one important meeting every second day), interaction with local parochial and public schools, social action programs, liturgical preparations, ecumenical relations, and the daily contacts through visitors and phone calls which cannot be planned in advance. Unless DRE's have carefully defined job descriptions (which most major dioceses by now have worked out), as well as carefully drawn up contracts (which most dioceses do not have as yet), all of the duties just mentioned may be assigned to them as a matter of course. They will also find themselves responsible, as many have done, for such extraneous roles as coach of the basketball team and general factotum.

Obviously, it is not possible for any one person to carry out all of these duties. What often occurs is a falling into them by default unless careful planning occurs before and during the Coordinator's stay in a particular parish community. The planning is the responsibility of the diocese or vicariate, the individual parish, and the person being hired. The plethora of duties presently devolving on individual DRE's is one of the strongest arguments for such planning, at the very least because of the human factors involved, and also one of the strongest arguments for the existence of teams of, rather than lone professionals, a movement already gaining much support in various parts of the country.

Another angle of vision one might bring toward clarification of the question of defining the Coordinator's role is to recognize that the question is both asked and answered from many points of view. Joseph Neiman points out at least four perspectives on the role,[4] namely, (1) the role at this time in history as generally viewed by the church; (2) the role as seen by peers, that is, the description of it when DRE's come together and talk with one another; (3) the role as prescribed and worked out in a

---

4. In *PACE*, Winona: St. Mary's College Press, December 1971, n.p.

given parish situation; and (4) the role as it is for a particular Coordinator, given her or his talent and personality. It is understandable that role confusion exists when one position can be looked at in so many different ways.

What has been said to this point has been meant to lead toward the locus or situation where DRE's find themselves today, the parish. In the next chapter, I should like to raise some questions about the parish, asking the reader to reflect specifically on her or his own situation as the questions are presented. Perhaps that organizational form, which seems so familiar, has changed more than we think.

STRATEGY NO. 1: THE DUTIES OF THE COORDINATOR

Separately, parish council, education committee, parish priests and coordinator are asked to list the duties they would require for their particular parish from a Coordinator-to-be or from one who is already working in the parish. The suggestion is made to list them in terms of the hours required, perhaps using some of the duties described in this chapter. It may also be possible to use the Anstep formula, with the combination for the three categories limited to fifteen. A working week of forty-five hours could thus be determined by multiplying the totals by three.

PARISH COUNCIL ASSESSMENT

THEOLOGY RESOURCE:

EDUCATION:

ADMINISTRATION:

EDUCATION COMMITTEE ASSESSMENT

THEOLOGY RESOURCE:

EDUCATION:

ADMINISTRATION:

PARISH CLERGY ASSESSMENT

THEOLOGY RESOURCE:

EDUCATION:

ADMINISTRATION:

DRE or COORDINATOR ASSESSMENT

THEOLOGY RESOURCE:

EDUCATION:

ADMINISTRATION:

2
Identifying Parish Dynamisms

In his preface to *Experience and Education*, John Dewey speaks of the necessity for the introduction of a new order of conceptions which will lead to new modes of practice. He admits the difficulties that arise when one starts working and conducting schools based on a new order, and agrees that it is much easier to walk in beaten paths.[1] A similar comment might be made with reference to the conduct of parishes. Until the fairly recent past, parishes worked well. Today, however, there is noticeable change, and one must pause to study what a new order of conceptions of the parish might include. Such is the purpose of this chapter.

Most people who work in parishes identify easily with David Hunter's comment in *Christian Education as Engagement* that planning takes time and if one is to plan well the most helpful steps to take are to (1) identify the situations giving rise to a need; (2) identify the dynamisms operating in the situations; (3) establish a set of strategies for coming to grips with these dynamisms; and (4) plan tactics and procedures.[2] I say that most people *agree* with the steps. But what most of us *do* is jump from one to four; we see a need and start planning, without taking into account the dynamisms.

This chapter will be concerned with dynamisms. The questions proposed are meant to help DRE's and other parish personnel clarify their own particular situations by processing the

---

1. John Dewey, *Experience and Education*, New York: The Macmillan Company, 1938, p. 5.
2. David Hunter, *Christian Education as Engagement*, New York: Seabury, 1963, p. 32.

information that could be gathered by considering questions about their parish together. Hopefully, these considerations will save time in the long run (saving time being the motivation usually pushing people to jump from #1 to #4) and be the foundation for strategies, tactics and procedures that will help parish personnel meet the needs of their individual situations.

QUESTION 1. *How do you distinguish between the real and the ideal parish?*

The question is triggered by a distinction Wilfred Cantwell Smith makes in *The Meaning and End of Religion*[3] where he notes that in speaking of our own religion or denomination, we tend to speak of it in ideal terms, while when looking at another group, we more easily note how it operates in the real world. For example, we may speak of ourselves ideally, in language such as "We are a pilgrim people, committed to the Lord, and to the service of others," while remarking of our brothers and sisters in other denominations, "Yes, there's a lot of talk about poverty, but just look at their property holdings."

The question is important for several reasons. First, it helps us to carve a vision for the future. Actually, parishes are probably always in tension between the real and the ideal. They would hope to be a community of people committed to the Lord, but they are as troubled by factions, money worries, personalities that don't mesh and sociological pressures as any other organization in today's world. It is a sign of humility and of realism when the tension is realized, when it can be said in truth that we aren't always what we say we are, and in the long run gives more credence to what we are trying to do.

Secondly, the question helps to get at one of the underlying causes for any argument. Sometimes when a discussion of the role of the parish is on the floor, there really is *not* disagreement: instead, the participants are speaking out of different frameworks. One may be speaking of the parish ideally, the other in its human and fragile state. It might be noted here that,

---

3. New York: New American Library Mentor Book, 1964, p. 48.

with reference to arguments, it is very difficult to have a genuine disagreement. Before I can know that I really don't see things as you do, I have to be quite clear about how you *do* see them. I have to get into your shoes and see what you see. Perhaps what I see when I really look is that we aren't actually arguing; we are simply looking at the same point from differing angles of vision.

This underscores the tremendous need for clear and simple language. Church people are notoriously prone, along with government and the military, to use jargon. The "maximum feasible capability" of Pentagon fame can easily be substituted with "a group of people encountering Christ in a transcendent setting, called by Him to charismatic and eschatological witness." The problem is especially acute when those educated in the field of theology, which includes most DRE's and clergy, carry on a conversation on religious matters with typical parishioners, whose language is shaped by *Time, Newsweek, People Magazine* and Walter Cronkite. It is a rare parish where only one language system operates.

Another reason for asking the question is canon law. Most adult Catholics in this country, while not students of canon law, learned long ago that to have a parish there are four requisites: a specific district, a specific people (i.e., Catholics, which if carried to the extreme causes some sort of problem where a Catholic is married to someone not a Catholic), a church building, and a pastor. At present all four are in trouble: boundaries between parishes become more and more blurred yearly, not only Catholics are among communicants in a given parish, communities meet and celebrate the Eucharist in a variety of settings, and a pastor in many places is the last one to find out this is happening, unless he, and it is still a he, is part of a team. Nevertheless, the canonical understanding of parish continues and the response to "What is really meant by parish?" unconsciously contains at least the remnants of these four elements.

QUESTION 2. *What is the image (picture) of the parish that makes the most sense to you?*

If one were to ask parishioners what picture of "parish"

came to their minds when one said that word, one could receive quite a lot of helpful feedback. For concrete realities, like church and parish, our minds do tend to respond with some kind of picture, not unlike the process that occurs in a word-association test. The point of asking the question here is to get at the plurality of pictures conjured up by any typical group of parish members. What, for example, would be the consensus from the point of view of senior citizens? How would the thirty-forty age group respond? What about the people under ten? Just asking the question helps the DRE and other parish personnel to understand that there is not one image that overrides the thinking of their parishioners. The response is thus in tandem with the question previous to this one.

However, there is some possibility that if the answer tends to be hazy, the parish is moving. If ambiguity has intruded its helpful head, the understanding has begun to grow among parish members, "No, it isn't exactly that; there's more (or less) to what we've been thinking of as parish." Writers in the field of ecclesiology[4] have proposed many images in recent years—servant, pilgrim people, institution, community—but the images will probably not become operative until the actuality can be demonstrated and pointed to. Raising the question here is not intended as a direction to take a position for one image as superior to others, but to point out their diversity. However, once there is acknowledgment of ambiguity, there is possibility of genuine renewal.

Most critical for a new image of parish is the question of size. One thinks easily of big city parishes of four and five thousand families, or of rural parishes where several hundred persons are spread over a large geographic area, and the general tendency is to try to divide them into smaller units. That movement is valid, but the important point would be to make the units very small, twenty-five or thirty people, interacting as communal units with one another. It is not bigness itself that is

---

4. See, for example, Avery Dulles, *Models of the Church*, New York: Doubleday, 1974. Dulles cites five models: institution, community, sacrament, herald, servant.

the problem, but how the smaller units interacting with the larger ones are structured. Neighborhood units would be a start, but so would interest units and family units. One thinks immediately of the DRE's community of teachers and their families as several natural units. The hidden, and explosive, factor then becomes the need for liturgical celebrants for smaller units. It is not unheard of that small communities *are* celebrating without ordained ministers, but the systemic question is one that is of enormous proportions, and will be returned to in later chapters.

QUESTION 3. *What do you see as the main cultural and sub-cultural influences affecting the parish in the next twenty-five years?*

Here, again, no attempt will be made to say, "These are the ones." However, some examples of cultural questions that immediately come to mind are those of communication, the changing pattern of authority, and the movement for the liberation of women (and men).[5] All of these will undoubtedly be affecting the parish critically in the future; in fact, they are already doing so, which calls for the necessity of viewing them now. The failure to look carefully at what is happening has always caused decline and confusion, because it has kept alive dying models until too late.

Communication, to take one example, has radically changed in our world. Some time ago, Harvey Cox noted that the only form of one-way communication left with us is preaching.[6] One might be tempted to ask "What about newscasters?" yet even there, most recently, the newscaster of any major story is generally asked a few questions by someone else on the news team after her or his report. The alternative is not necessarily the dialogue homily; it might be better to suggest the elimination of preaching in order to be drawn into the language and ac-

---

5. The reader is invited to cite her or his own choices: cultural referring to the wider society; sub-cultural to one's own situation where specific economic, racial, ethnic, and educational factors may be extremely important.

6. The comment does not apply to many black churches.

tivity of the Eucharistic ritual itself. We have become so talk-
ative in churches that we forget how powerful and vital non-verbal communication can be. Here the young can teach us a great
deal by their understanding of ritual. No one needs to explain to
a little child what to do during the kiss of peace.

The changing nature of authority is another cultural influence affecting the parish. The question is not so much "What
did we do wrong?" as "What is it we once did that is no longer
appropriate?" The very real change in patterns of information
flow, decision making and budget planning in all other contemporary institutions will probably cause changes in the parish
structure of authority not through resistance, but because, more
and more, people will not be able to function in a top to middle
to bottom pattern. If, in all the other communities and organizations to which they belong, people have a voice and a vote,
the parish will be forced to move to a more communitarian
style.

As yet, the women's movement has not really been of primary concern in Catholicism. Individual women are organizing
here and there, but if one looks at the membership of societies
within the larger church such as the Canon Law Society and the
Catholic Theological Society of America, if one looks at the
faculties of major church-related universities (except those
staffed by religious orders of women), if one simply looks into
the sanctuary on Sunday, one sees very few women. Of course
the major church position in Catholicism is still one open only
to men. That this will change is hardly debatable, but just when
the change will begin in earnest is still a matter of conjecture.
Possibly the greatest source of hope for the future of this movement rests with religious orders of women, who seem to be
more and more free from and resistant to the ecclesiastical re-
straints which for so many years kept them in the position of
minors.

QUESTION 4. *What are the attitudes within the parish to
sex, to power, and to money?*
The first question extends the women's question previously

cited, but is intended to zero in on the roles women and men are called to play in the parish, as well as their functions in parish activities. Are the parish roles assigned on the basis of sex? Who are the behind the scenes people, and who are the people out front? What is the attitude in the parish toward working mothers or toward professional women and men who are not married? Are there any programs directed to them? What of the parish's responsibility to its divorced Catholics? And can the question of homosexuality even be raised, and the parish challenged toward some kind of ministry to those of its members in this group?

Power and money are different questions, but they can be placed together at least as far as the comment that it is critical in any parish to find out who makes and implements the decisions, whose "say" is crucial to an issue, and who decides where the money goes. Here diocesan and episcopal pressures must be considered as well. The automatic taxing of individual parishes for diocesan projects does not always take into consideration whether such projects are of importance to all the people in a diocese. Church people are very often uneasy when questions of power are raised; power is too often looked upon as force. Yet genuine power is the fullness of human energy directed toward the betterment of the universe, the power of the heart surgeon, the poet, and the saint. Before one makes conclusions on the decision making question posed above, then, the more important issue in the parish might be the coming to grips with an understanding of the nature of human power, and a marshaling of the humanizing energies within the parish toward those activities the church speaking ideally usually attributes to herself: feeding the hungry, clothing the naked and comforting the oppressed.

If religious people shy away from questions of power, money questions are even more problematical; they certainly start as many, if not more, disagreements. How many parishes, for example, have been bitterly divided over the percent of the budget spent on the parochial school, causing the question of the existence and nature of the school to be put aside, as well as whether it is performing critical educational tasks.[7] Secondly, why are parish ministers so often the financial role-takers, cutting down on the time that might be more valuably spent in pastoral work? Any parish has within its congregation many persons who could take on the financial business of the parish, or, better, enough persons to form finance committees representative of all parish interests, which could develop new and ingenious approaches to fund raising and spending. One litmus test: What percentage of the parish budget automatically goes to the poor?

QUESTION 5. *What is the nature of the relationships between people in the parish? What are the relationships?*

One begins to see here how the questions that are being raised overlap. For example, do the CCD people and the parochial school people work together out of a common educational philosophy? Do working groups in the parish meet once a month for a particular reason and then separate, or do they initially begin their interaction with a weekend or all-day meeting somewhere outside of their immediate environment? Do they pray together, other than at Sunday Mass? How involved are the people in the creation of their liturgies together?[8]

The question is particularly directed to the role-personal identity distinction formulated by Erik Erikson,[9] and refers particularly to the more visible roles in the parish. Is the pastor always "the pastor" or is he sometimes free to be Joe or Pete or Harry? Is the principal of the school, if there is a school, "the principal" or, again, someone to be related to as herself or himself? Similarly, is there the parish coordinator, the parish council president, and the assistant pastor or pastors? These are the

---

7. This question is asked from the perspective of a person who although professionally a "religious educator" has recently completed a year as principal of a Catholic school which was a symbol of hope to all involved with it.

8. For an ideal parish example of this, one might cite St. Therese Parish in Cresskill, New Jersey.

9. In *Childhood and Society*, New York: W. W. Norton, 1950, pp. 261-263.

people who are generally the topic of conversation when relationships in the parish are discussed, and the kind of negative criticism that sometimes is directed toward them is often a result of people seeing them *only* in their one most visible parish role, rather than in the variety of roles that human beings play: friend, sister, brother, listener, comforter, parent, and spouse.

Finally, are decisions made at the appropriate level in the parish, or is there some ultimate veto power that one person possesses in function of a role? A great many necessary decisions are not made in parishes simply because someone is afraid of consequences. Thus the status quo gets another boost, and the possibility of learning through healthy failure, as well as the probability that new life will be engendered, is never attempted. One caution: although DRE's and those in other major parish roles would do well to go ahead and make decisions they see as necessary, it is always helpful to keep in mind David Appleby's caution: When you make a decision, you should know beforehand the answer to four questions: Who's going to be mad? How mad? Who's going to be glad? How glad?

QUESTION 6. *Is there any shift toward a rearrangement of the traditional categories of priests, nuns and lay persons in the parish?*

In most parishes, there are identifiable people who are the priests, others who are the nuns (or "the good sisters" as preachers are fond of addressing them) and the people. There are human and semantic problems here—for example, where does one place religious orders of brothers?—as well as deeply underlying attitudes toward the nature of priesthood, religion and laos. One human problem surfacing more and more in parishes is the presence of many people who have been in several of the categories. More than one active minister has commented on the waste of talent and training in his parish where there may be five or ten ex-priests (or, as one former brother more kindly puts it, "those who have retired from the organization").

Again, it is the language here that is significant of genuine change. Theological and ecclesiological commentators have long spoken of the entire people as "priestly" but the recent change is that many people are now involved in doing priestly things and speaking of these things as such. Parish Coordinators, especially, speak of their work as ministry, as do campus personnel, health workers and counselors. If ministry is the work of all, and if by ministry is meant doing what priests have done as well as continuing to perform the spiritual and corporal works of mercy, then not only the terminology is in question, but so is the reality itself. Perhaps it is even true that everyone is a priest at least part of the time. More significant is its correlative: no one is a priest all of the time. Priest is not something one becomes, but an activity carried on within a religious community. Similarly, one is not "a" religious; religious describes each person in the community. So too does the designation of each parish member as one who is of the "laos." In some sense, no one is priest, religious or lay; in another, everyone is called to be priestly, religious and people.

QUESTION 7. *What is the quality of worship in the parish?*

In a sense, the answer to this question is determined by all of the other responses. However, it depends primarily on whether the parish is a community or, perhaps better, a community of communities. Worship always grows out of the nature of a people's life together, and attempts at patching up the liturgy do not always get at examination of deeper issues.

It would seem to be valid, if some in the community wished it, to have many styles of worship, designed to accommodate the varieties of styles of prayer that people engage in. Most parishes have devoted much care to liturgies that satisfy the young, through what has come to be referred to as the "folk Mass." One is still hard put, however, to find parishes actively involved in liturgies meant for the wide diversity of parishioners found everywhere. People whose worship lives are more sustained by silence and an atmosphere of stillness have sometimes discovered the only way to achieve this is to pray on their own. Others find worship with a group of several hundred strangers, seated face to back, almost intolerable.

What must be remarked here is that such attitudes are not necessarily divisive, and people in parishes infected with liturgical inertia need to question whether they have a responsibility toward those whose worship lives are not presently being nourished.

There are three other questions, but each of them deserves a chapter of its own, since each is so closely tied to the work of the DRE. Question 8, "What is the parish theory of organization?" will be addressed in chapter four. Question 9, "What is the philosophy of education operating in the parish?" will underlie the considerations in chapters seven, eight and nine. Question 10 will be the consideration of the last chapter of this book. It is: Out of what religious or theological stance does the parish function? This last question threads its way in and out of most of what is being considered here, but like the questions of organization and education, it is rarely asked explicitly. It is toward the explication of these questions, and the working through of some of the suggested tactics and procedures for dealing with them, that the rest of this book is directed.

STRATEGY NO. 2: NEEDS AND THE PARISH

The following strategy on parish needs takes much time and thought. It might serve as the basis for reflection or the agenda for an overnight parish staff meeting, or as the basis of the parish council's consideration over a year-long period, as might all of the questions forming the substance of this chapter.

A. The following questions require a simple yes or no answer. In each case, however, you are requested to give a one sentence rationale for the response you make.

  1. Does the parish need to be involved in the education of children?

  2. Does the parish need to be involved in the education of adolescents?

  3. Does the parish need to be involved in the education of adults?

  4. Does the parish need to be involved in social justice?

  5. Does the parish need to be involved in problems of poverty, housing, war, prison reform?

  6. Does the parish need to be involved in political life?

B. Given the areas of need you chose for the parish tasks, how would you allocate parish financial resources on a percentage basis?

Given the areas of need you chose, how would you allocate parish personnel resources on a percentage basis?

Given the areas of need you chose, how would you allocate the resources of the physical plant of the parish on a percentage basis?

C. Would you see any need for a revision of decision making power in the parish if there were a consensus concerning revision of priorities in the parish?

What revisions would you suggest?

How might they be effected and implemented?

This is an interesting questionnaire to administer according to age groups, for example:

people under 10
people 10-15
people 15-20
people 20-30
people 30-40

people 40-50
people 50-60
people 60-70
people 70-80
people 80 and up

STRATEGY NO. 3: THE INDIVIDUAL NEED AND THE PARISH

1. If you could keep only one thing about your parish, what would it be?

2. What do you like best about your parish?

3. What do you see as the greatest sign of hope in your parish?

4. If you could change one thing about your parish, what would it be?

5. What do you like least about your parish?

6. What do you see as the one greatest need in your parish over the next five years?

3
What Is a Coordinator?

In the first chapter, it was suggested that the term "Coordinator" is an ambiguous one. Another way of saying this is that the term Coordinator is susceptible to many interpretations. Two interpretations are familiar, but each raises further questions. The first is that a Coordinator is one who co-orders, causes to work or act together harmoniously (Webster), or brings together an ordering of realities. In a parish, this might mean educational and theological or religious realities. It also indicates that as soon as one asks "What is a Coordinator?" one realizes that this is not the first question. For the answer to this, if the phrase "Parish Coordinator" has any meaning, is that the Coordinator coordinates the parish. Hence the design of chapter two, where we paused to look at the question of the parish as our starting point.

However, this is not *actually* what the Coordinator does, that is, coordinate the parish. If anyone is engaged in this task, it is more likely that it is a group composed of clergy, school personnel and parish society representatives. More than likely, the question has little meaning because in actuality no one has reflected too seriously on the use of the term "Parish Coordinator." Perhaps there is a vague uneasiness that it doesn't quite fit, but generally the question is not brought to consciousness or articulation.

The uneasiness about the appellation is the major reason for the second and interchangeable title: DRE. The Coordinator's province generally is not the entire parish; he or she has been hired because there is a religious education program in existence, or there is a proposal for one to come into existence. Someone is needed to "run" it. But because "runner of the religious education program" is not only cumbersome but linguistically impotent, the operative verb is "direct." Someone must "direct" the program. Hence the term DRE—a bit more accurate than Coordinator, but hardly inclusive or comprehensive enough.[1]

Neither of these, then, is a precise term, but the reader is invited to (a) accept this; (b) live with it as an operative fact; (c) consider in the following pages those activities in which the DRE is most engaged, and strive with her or his peers to find a professional handle that might sometime in the future become not only the accepted but the truest description of the role, as well as an answer to the inquiry "What is a Coordinator?" The questions which follow are intended to lead us in that direction.

QUESTION 1. *How is the nature of leadership viewed in the parish?*

The Coordinator is accepted as one of the parish leaders. But what is the meaning of the term "leader"? Some time ago, in working with a group of Parish Coordinators in Rockville Centre, New York, I asked the question in another way as the closing reflection in one of a series of weekly seminars for parish leaders. As posed, the question was to think of the important qualities a Coordinator should possess as a parish leader. The following week, before our meeting began, one Coordinator, a mature, educated gentleman who had spent a career in publishing, reported to the group that he had been thinking of the question all week and had decided on his answer. We asked him to share it with us. Without hesitation, he responded firmly: "There are five qualities. Number one: imagination. Number two: imagination. Number three: imagination. Number four: Imagination. And, number five: IMAGINATION."

That response was provocative, and illustrative of an educational process. Rather than researching the meaning of leadership and accepting past definitions without reflection, we

---

1. Direct can mean many things: cause a person or thing to turn, move, point or follow a certain course; regulate; control; guide; command; correct.

should perhaps search for our own answers together as learners. To take another example, several years ago when religious orders first started asking "subjects" to submit the names of possible "superiors" and to cite the reasons, one Sister responded with several names, but with only one qualification: anyone to be placed in a position of leadership must be someone who is not easily threatened. It might be added that the correlative is equally true: a leader, ideally, is not only not easily threatened; he or she does not easily threaten others.

In *The New Community*, Gabriel Moran makes a further wise observation about leadership. While pointing out that the entire concept of leader may have a certain invalidity, suggesting as it does a non-communitarian spatial distance between leader and led, he does write:

> The ideal leader is the one who is strong enough to keep turning power back to each person at his own level. The next best leader may be the weak one who unintentionally brings other people to make decisions for themselves. The worst kind of leader today is one who is only partially incompetent. He works diligently at being a good leader, which is perhaps the worst way to be a leader.[2]

The point that I wish to make here is that the concept of leader is not easily describable, and that the task of trying to do so may be a fruitless one. A better criterion may be to look at what people accomplish when a leader, so-called, is present. Robert Townsend seems to favor this approach. In *Up the Organization*, he indicates that leadership is a composite of qualities desired *from* a particular someone and brought *by* that particular someone. He observes that leaders come in all different shapes and sizes and have varied personalities, that some are mediocre and some bright, and that no one set of characteristics will perfectly describe the ideal leader. Yet he does conclude that one may be aware that leadership is present from the kind of performances the people working with the leader turn in.

---

2. New York: Herder and Herder, 1970, p. 92.

Quoting Lao-Tzu, he recalls the advice, "To lead the people, walk behind them," adding:

> As for the best leaders, the people do not notice their existence. The next best, the people honor and praise. The next, the people fear; and the next, the people hate. . . . When the best leader's work is done the people say, "We did it ourselves!"[3]

It seems to me that this may be the aspect of leadership most consonant with the aims of the Parish Coordinator. He or she works with groups of people and has as an objective the realization of the kind of community where all participate as fully as possible in the community's activities. Perhaps the Coordinator's best work is done, not when she or he has put herself or himself out of a job, but when the community is running so smoothly that people do not notice, and all say to one another, "Ah! We did this ourselves."

QUESTION 2. *Is the Coordinator a member of a team?*

It is important to raise this question, since many Coordinators speak of themselves as being members of a pastoral team. Let us begin by addressing the first word in this phrase, "pastoral." The question certainly has to be raised whether pastoral, coming as it does from the term for shepherd, is anachronistic and inappropriate in a non-agricultural society. However, as used today, the term is intended to convey the fact that DRE's see themselves as primarily involved in an effort that is devoted to helping people in very direct and personal ways. These include what used to be referred to as the spiritual and corporal works of mercy—instructing the ignorant, counseling the doubtful, comforting the sorrowful, bearing wrongs patiently, forgiving all injuries, praying for the living and dead, admonishing the sinner (or, as Jean Cruttenden observes, "confronting with charity"), feeding the hungry, giving drink to the thirsty, sheltering the homeless, clothing the naked, visiting the imprisoned and

---

3. New York: Knopf, 1970, pp. 88-89.

the sick, and burying the dead—works demanded of all who would think of themselves as church members.[4]

Coordinators usually are hired for only one of these, which in an expression that is far too limited is "instructing the ignorant," and more appropriately phrased as "educating" or "educating in the area of religion." If there is a team doing such work, the work divisions are almost always along age lines. For example, given a team of three, one directs religious education with children, one with teenagers, one with adults. Another way this is handled is by relying on the specific training of team members and then planning programs in accordance with it. A broader kind of activity results, for example, if a team has four members trained, respectively, in sociology, psychology, education and religious studies; more specific activity is carried on by members trained in morality, scripture, doctrine and pedagogy.

The word "pastoral," however, has wider application than this, and in practice the Parish Coordinator does tend to move into other than educational activities. He or she, or they, often find that parish visiting must be a facet of the profession, and the works of mercy alluded to above carried on as a matter of course. The main connotation of pastoral, however, comes in the connections the DRE has personally as a team member with parish clergy, and professionally, as one involved in sacramental and liturgical activity. It is here that the critical change is occurring, it is here that the new kind of co-official in the church is emerging; it is here that ministry and priesthood are going through the greatest changes on the grass roots level. If a Coordinator meets regularly with parish clergy, if he or she is an equal in planning, deliberating, counseling and decision making, if the Coordinator is intimately involved in liturgy, the question is due to surface sooner or later: Just what is the difference between ordained and non-ordained?

This is precisely why one must pause to examine the other word in the phrase "pastoral team." The Coordinator who speaks of being on a team is not just engaged in word play or in

---

4. In the wider society, the categories used are health, education and welfare.

a more equitable work arrangement. However, the conclusion that one is on a team is one that may be both naive and premature. For one is *not* a team member unless there is equality across the board. One criterion is financial: Are salaries and benefits equal for equal work, whether the team member is a cleric, a member of a religious order, or a lay person? Another is in the area of decision making. Is there anyone who has a final say when decisions are to be made, or does the decision making power reside corporately in the group? A third and more subtle criterion is the attitude of non-team members toward the so-called team. That is, do parishioners on the one hand, and representatives of the official church on the other, recognize the existence of a team, or are there one or several persons regarded as actually in charge, while the others are co-workers, but not co-equals? Finally, is there division along sexist lines, so that women are not taken seriously as partners?

The answers to these questions may be taken as indicative of whether a team truly exists, or if, in actuality, one is really a member of a pastoral staff. A team is a horizontal and communitarian unit; a staff is vertical and usually hierarchical. It takes a long time for a genuine team to come into existence, to operate as such and to be recognized by the community as a reality. That time may not yet be here, but there are signs everywhere that it is coming. It is a radical, a root change, one to be reflected upon and entered into with awareness of the possible conclusions. For when genuine teams do exist in parishes, Catholics in this country may find out that they are members of a new kind of church.

QUESTION 3. *What kind of a change agent is the Coordinator?*

This question assumes that the Coordinator is some kind of agent for change, since the act of hiring a Coordinator is itself a shift in any given parish. Change agents, however, may, like leaders, come in various shapes and sizes. What might be of assistance to a Coordinator in self-assessment, or to a parish in making a choice of a DRE, would be a brief consideration of some of the most frequently cited characteristics of change agents.[5]

At one end of the continuum are those who may be thought of as Innovators. One who is an Innovator is likely to assume risks easily, to adopt new practices, to adapt them to local needs, and to provide trial for new procedures. In one study, Lionberger found that Innovators are among the first 2 ½ % to adopt a new practice[6] and it is therefore understandable that they are often regarded as questionable deviants in some communities. In consequence, the Innovator is someone who needs a support group composed of many formal and informal contacts outside the immediate community. He or she will generally have graduate and professional school education, and will tend to be somewhat younger than other kinds of change agents.

Not everyone's psyche is geared toward being an Innovator; there is a peculiar kind of strength and personality operative here. Therefore, not every Coordinator will function best in this role, particularly if there is no strong support group to be relied upon. Further, one's personality may not include the tolerance for high risk or the ability to live on the cutting edge characteristic of the Innovator. Neither is every parish ready for one. Parishes and groups within parishes will have different abilities for coping with change and will be at different stages of readiness in the process that leads toward the acceptance of change. Thus, unless some of the pre-conditions for the presence of an Innovator exist, her or his work may be damaging and fruitless. There is need then for the presence of a second kind of change agent, the Legitimator.

Legitimators have broader social orientations than Innovators, although they too are generally better educated and receptive to new ideas. However, their special gifts lie in the ability they have to help dispel fears about innovations, to evaluate innovations in terms of their own situations, and to select and in-

---

5. See Herbert Lionberger, *Adoption of New Ideas and Practices*, Ames: Iowa State University Press, 1960, esp. pp. 52-66.
6. *Ibid.*, p. 53.

terpret information, incorporating both positive and negative recommendations. In the community, they are highly accessible for advice, tend to be informally recognized as molders of opinion, and serve as reinforcers of decisions already made. It might be pointed out here that one is not necessarily a pure "type." One may combine the characteristics of Innovator and Legitimator as well as the vitally necessary functions of the third kind of change agent, the Communicator.

The Communicator is of prime necessity in the dissemination of information about change. It is not particularly important whether a Communicator is for or against a change; what is important is that she or he has wide and varied contacts, great social accessibility, and the trust of the community. In addition, a communicator has a personal antenna that is sensitive to the presence of change, and is open to and interested in new ideas, at least as ideas. The Communicator, upon being informed of something new, is inclined to want to discuss it, and, in bouncing ideas off other persons, provides necessary dissemination of information, without particularly influencing the hearer's evaluative reaction.

It is the function of the fourth kind of change agent, the Skeptic, to precipitate some kind of evaluation of change. Skeptic at times has a negative connotation but the positive importance of this role cannot be stressed too strongly. On the one hand, the Skeptic is the clarifier, the one who prods the Innovator and Legitimator to think through ideas and practices, retranslate, simplify and realize. On the other hand, the Skeptic can prevent the making of costly mistakes. Any parish without resident Skeptics is in for deep trouble; myriad ills from fuzzy thinking to head-on plunges in the wrong direction can be avoided when he or she is present.

Most Coordinators and parish personnel will probably find themselves acting as all four of these at one time or another. Nevertheless, it is likely that one will be a predominant mode of activity. All four are necessary, and if a parish is moving in the direction of positive change, the only kind, since non-change is impossible and negative change a hindrance, then all four are to be sought out, cultivated, and affirmed.

QUESTION 4. *How does the Coordinator function at meetings?*

This question is a major one since meetings take so much of the time of parish personnel. In the chapter on Time Management, the nature and purpose of meetings as well as consideration of ways of holding them will be addressed; here I am interested in raising the question of the Coordinator's style at meetings, the question of style being one more way of answering "What is a Coordinator?"

A familiar distinction in works on group process is that between task and maintenance. If a group meets, it ostensibly does so for a particular purpose, or to accomplish some job: this is its *task*. In addition, human interaction is the mode of operation when a group is meeting. If there is to be communication, there is need for the members to be engaged with and by one another, to cooperate, and to exist *as a group*, but with regard for individual members. This is called *maintenance*.

Since Coordinators have almost daily meetings, it is helpful for them to examine whether they are more inclined to be task or maintenance persons, and, if so, in which task or maintenance activity they are most involved. It is also important for them to realize that all the activities of task and maintenance need to go on if a group meeting is to be successful. They must therefore be aware of and provide for activities in both categories, something possible to do once they reflect carefully on just what it is they *do* do at meetings. One helpful tool for a DRE here is a tape recorder. To analyze one's style at a meeting, the DRE can listen to the taped record, which will indicate without too much distortion the kinds of moves, questions and responses he or she normally makes.

One way of categorizing task activities is to see them as either initiating, regulating or informing. The activity of initiating can be observed in the offering of a new direction, the asking of a new question, calling for or giving definition, or suggesting a new way in which a topic can be viewed. Such phrases as, "Another possibility would be . . .", or "I wonder if we might look at it this way . . .", or "Could someone help clarify this point for me . . . ?" are typical initiating phrases.

A second task activity is regulating. Generally, this is the work of a chairperson, but at small, informal meetings, it is a task sometimes glossed over or poorly performed. If the Coordinator is not chairing the meeting, it may be helpful for her or him to be sure that regulating activities are going on, that is, that someone is responsible for preparing an agenda, that the business of the meeting is being covered, that when and if the group wanders it is brought back to the topic, and that summarizing occurs periodically and fruitless discussions are either tabled or terminated. Tact is essential for the regulating activity —tact and timing—and the cultivation of competence in both puts invaluable tools into the hands of the Coordinator.

Informing is the third task activity, and it includes the offering of necessary data, provision of tables and statistics, sharing of details of programs already completed, and reporting on proposed actions. It is difficult to classify informing solely as a task function, since its importance for group maintenance is so great. For example, how much friction might be prevented in parishes if memoranda and newsletters were not only kept up to date, explicitly and carefully written, and acknowledged and read when received? How much repetition would be avoided at meetings if informing were more of an art? And how many more times might a simple informing mechanism beforehand, a phone call perhaps, have precluded the dangerous phrase so often, and unfortunately, heard at meetings, "But nobody ever told me that"—a killer phrase that has for all practical purposes ended many meetings before the actual business was concluded and tuned out those whose participation was most necessary?

As distinguished from task, maintenance activities are more concerned with the human processes of the group members, and with the affect aspect of the meeting. The main one may be termed "supporting." This word is intended to capture the nature of an activity by which someone in the group makes sure that everyone is heard from, listened to, and given enough time. It also carries with it the opposite and more delicate activity of seeing that no one dominates or takes too much time, a problem parliamentarians often deal with by setting a definite limit for statements (4-5 minutes) and Parish Coordinators meet by using a simple kitchen timer. Supporting is also directed toward drawing out opinions and comments from less vocal members, sensing the difference between genuine disagreements and unclarified language, and seeing that the issue, and not the person addressing the issue, is the focus of attention. This may mean in one instance encouragement of ideas, in another resolution of conflict through a request for rephrasing, or, in a third, a call for a five-minute break to either defuse or refuel.

The last group activity, also one of maintenance, is evaluating. The word evaluating admits of several meanings, and will be returned to in more detail in chapter seven, when educational valuing will be discussed. At a meeting, however, it is that activity signified by such questions as "Do we want to act on this suggestion?" "Do we have enough information to make a decision?" "Has everyone who wishes to addressed the issue?" "Shall we conclude now?" Evaluating as an activity is designed to help the group clarify its objectives and its reasons for meeting, as well as to assess whether these have been accomplished in fact. One simple way of evaluating a group's reaction to a meeting is to give out a questionnaire after the meeting, to be returned as soon as possible, asking only two questions: (1) Do you think this meeting was necessary? and (2) Why or why not?

QUESTION 5. *To what extent is the Coordinator called upon for an attitude of creativity?*

Creativity is one of the least understood yet most necessary attitudes for people if they are to live up to their human potential. It is not always cultivated by our United States educational system, and when it is, it is more likely to be associated with children than with adults. In the following pages, I would like to address it, as Erich Fromm does, as an attitude appropriate to any human activity, and recognizable by several distinctive features.[7] These features are as apparent or absent in a DRE as in anyone else.

---

7. See "The Creative Attitude," in *Creativity and Its Cultivation*, Harold H. Anderson, ed., New York: Harper and Row, 1959, pp. 45-54.

The first sign of the creative attitude, says Fromm, is the capacity to be puzzled. The Coordinator who asks "Why not?" instead of "Why?" is likely to possess it. This capacity is signified by such phrases as "I wonder if . . . ." and "Suppose . . . ." But it is the aspect of puzzlement that is central. Coordinators need desperately to *not* know all the answers, to be searchers for reasons under reasons, and to enter parishes and live in their work there with the kind of stance that expects dilemmas, paradoxes and mysteries to abound far more than answers or solutions. In a parish, this is particularly true for two reasons. The first is that it is the parish's *religious* life in which the Coordinator is involved, and this is an area of life touched and surrounded by mystery, where one always takes off one's shoes, remembering that the ground is holy. The second is that most parishioners have more than enough "answers," so-called, while too few have worked through the questions. Questions, genuine questions, are puzzles, not ultimately without solution, but intricate enough to involve time, wrong turns, humor and an Aha! conclusion. If Coordinators could convey to their sister and brother parishioners that they are co-puzzlers in reflecting on the riddle of life, an attitude of creativity could grow in the parish.

The ability to concentrate is another sign of creativity. Concentration is a needed quality whenever any work is to be done well; it is the human corrective against fragmentation, and a focusing ability that helps keep us whole and integral. Here the particular focus I should like to stress is the Coordinator's attitude of prayer. To be con-centered means to be able to exist with a center; when things fall apart, as well as when people fall apart, it is the center that does not hold. Coordinators need to know how to be in touch with their own centers of being, with that part of themselves most available through prayer. But concentrate also implies being with the other centers, with the other persons, or, put in religious terms, in community. The ability to concentrate is, then, a requisite for anyone who would seek to foster parish community.

A third requisite for the creative attitude is the experience of the I, the experience of initiating and being responsible for one's own person and one's own activities. Here is an aspect of the creative attitude much threatened whenever one is in a highly visible role. Very often, the temptation is to try to live up to the expectations of others rather than live up to one's own, attempting at the extreme to be an amalgam, a composite of stereotyped characteristics, rather than one's own best self. As with the perfect girl or boy scout, the perfect Coordinator is patient, kind, courteous, obedient and loyal. The DRE who experiences her or his own I, however, realizes that this may not always be possible, and settles not for the arrogance of "the one way which is my way," but for the humility that is the best I can possibly be in these circumstances.

Familiar to any DRE are the conflict and tension which result from polarity. Fromm writes that the ability to accept such conflict and tension is a sign of the creative attitude. At this time in parishes throughout the United States, polarity is evident in varying degrees almost everywhere. At its worst, it breeds hatred, suspicion and division; at its best, healthy argument and intensified study. To be creative in the midst of such polarity does not require premature solution; it does suggest, however, as Tillich once said, the ability to live with the possibility of failure where solutions are tried as well as the possibility that at present there may not be viable solutions.

> If there is no solution, then no premature solutions should be tried; rather, the human situation in its conflicts should be expressed courageously. If it is expressed, it is already transcended. He who can bear guilt and express guilt shows that he already knows about 'acceptance-in-spite-of'. He who can bear and express meaninglessness shows that he experiences meaning within his own desert of meaninglessness.[8]

Richard Farson has written that we are not particularly good, in the United States, at stewing over our problems; our credo is:

---

8. Paul Tillich, *Theology of Culture,* New York: Oxford University Press, 1959, p. 75.

"It is better to light one candle than curse the darkness."[9] Creative Coordinators know how to do the latter: they are able not only to take time to stew over problems, but, when necessary, they are even comfortable cursing the darkness.

The last sign of the creative attitude is the willingness to be born every day. Here, puzzlement, concentration, the I, and polarities are brought together. For the willingness to be born again daily implies that one has died the day before yet risen again, that one has drawn strength from prayer and trusts one's own judgment, and that one's "I" has come to terms with polarity, tension and ambiguity. The Coordinator's work is not unique in calling for a daily rebirth, but the job itself is so new and the call for new programming, planning and vision so constant that a crucial state of mind and heart to be brought to it is, perhaps, this willingness to be born again.

QUESTION 6. *Can the Coordinator identify and provide the elements of restructuring? What are these elements?*

One of the qualities that might be ascribed to one who is a parish leader is the ability to figure out what is needed to start rebuilding an organization. De-struction has as its purpose the breaking down of some reality, with intent; in the church today, although this may be necessary in part, it is the restructuring of elements that is called for. These elements, and the stress on them needed by a particular parish will certainly vary, but the elements will undoubtedly include community, religion, education, administration and prayer. It is up to Coordinators to identify those specific to their own situations.

QUESTION 7. *How clear is the Coordinator's language?*

This question has been alluded to in chapter two; here it is asked of the individual Coordinator. The language peculiar to church people when they become hortatory and homiletical might best be described as "incensy," that is, language that sounds the way incense smells. If the Coordinator recalls the statistic often cited in educational literature that we recall 10%

---

9. In *Birthrights*, New York: Macmillan, 1974, esp. pp. 214-216.

of what we taste, touch and smell, 20% of what we hear, 30% of what we see, 50% of what we see and hear, 70% of what we ourselves put into language and 90% of what we discover for ourselves, the importance of this question may be sensed. The Coordinator is called on constantly not only to speak of religious matters (directed to only 20 or 30% of participant response), but to help others articulate their own understandings (the 70 and 90% end of the spectrum). Clarity and simplicity of speech then become essential. Any of us who are teachers are aware of the experience of hearing ourselves while teaching, and suddenly realizing that the words are unconnected to our bodies; it is the danger, the dis-embodied use of language, that I seek to point to here. Those who are Coordinators would do well to do as Robert Frost did, use words of three and four syllables sparingly, and five-syllable words hardly at all. If this is done, the Word Who is the Coordinator's primary referent may just possibly make Its presence known.

QUESTION 8. *Does the Coordinator have an organization of peers?*

The question is probably self-evident, but it is raised because so many Coordinators in this country do not have even informal peer groups. It is particularly directed to the need for the kind of support that can only come from someone who knows a work from the inside. Ideally, this would be other DRE's. There is need to come together with such persons at times, especially when there is difficulty. However, many other reasons exist. Where a team is not present in a particular parish, Coordinators from several parishes may form a team among themselves although each is based at a different location. This would help to prevent duplication of efforts and encourage thorough preparation. For example, in a teacher training program where each parish has a course in child psychology, pedagogy, scripture and doctrine, four Coordinators might agree that each will take one area, study and teach it in depth, and then provide extensive instruction in that one field in four parishes, instead of more limited instruction in four fields in one parish. One beneficial side effect: if the Coordinator is looked at askance, or as an

Innovator who is a questionable deviant, contact by parishioners with three others who do not seem quite as crazy can allay fears when and if they arise.

Questions 9 and 10 lead to our next two chapters, but it may be helpful to include them here. Question 9, "What are your goals and objectives?" will be addressed in chapter four, and Question 10, "Have you learned to manage time?" will be the subject of chapter five. Both of these questions are administrative ones, and the next three chapters will be concerned with this first of the three major areas of the Coordinator's work: organization and management.

STRATEGY NO. 4: RATE YOURSELF AS A CHANGE AGENT

On a scale of 1 to 5, 1 signifying *never*, 2 *rarely*, 3 *often*, 4 *more often than not*, and 5 *always*, assess the usual style you use as a change agent.

INNOVATOR:
I assume risks. (1 - 2 - 3 - 4 - 5)
I am first in my area to adopt new practices. (1 - 2 - 3 - 4 - 5)
I have many formal and informal outside contacts.
  (1 - 2 - 3 - 4 - 5)
I have been told I am a questionable deviant by several people.
  (1 - 2 - 3 - 4 - 5)
I have great mental flexibility. (1 - 2 - 3 - 4 - 5)

LEGITIMATOR:
I am exposed to sources of information outside my immediate
  locality. (1 - 2 - 3 - 4 - 5)
I am consistently receptive to new ideas. (1 - 2 - 3 - 4 - 5)
I am called on often to dispel fears about innovations.
  (1 - 2 - 3 - 4 - 5)
I am highly accessible for information and advice.
  (1 - 2 - 3 - 4 - 5)
I often reinforce decisions already made. (1 - 2 - 3 - 4 - 5)

COMMUNICATOR:
I have wide social accessibility. (1 - 2 - 3 - 4 - 5)
I have many contacts with outside sources of information.
  (1 - 2 - 3 - 4 - 5)
I tend to share information with others, particularly if it is new
  to me. (1 - 2 - 3 - 4 - 5)
I am looked on in the community as conservative of traditional
  values. (1 - 2 - 3 - 4 - 5)
I usually seek new ideas and am familiar with varied sources of
  information. (1 - 2 - 3 - 4 - 5)

SKEPTIC:

I am generally slow to adopt new suggestions. (1 - 2 - 3 - 4 - 5)
I insist on more than average evidence. (1 - 2 - 3 - 4 - 5)
I require much time to think over new ideas. (1 - 2 - 3 - 4 - 5)
I tend to equate new ideas in terms of tangible probable results.
(1 - 2 - 3 - 4 - 5)
I find my usual style is to raise questions about new practices
more than my colleagues do. (1 - 2 - 3 - 4 - 5)

STRATEGY NO. 5: DISCOVERING YOUR STYLE
AT MEETINGS

1. Tape two or three meetings in which you have recently participated.
2. List the comments, questions and observations you personally have made at these meetings.
3. Categorize these contributions under the appropriate heading:

INITIATING:

REGULATING:

INFORMING:

SUPPORTING:

EVALUATING:

STRATEGY NO. 6: ASSESSING PEER ORGANIZATION. AN AGENDA FOR BREAKFAST SEMINARS

Due to the irregular scheduling of the parish activities in which Coordinators are involved, a meeting time that is generally acceptable for most is the morning. One way to refer to such morning meetings is as Breakfast Seminars. These Breakfast Seminars have the advantage of occurring at the time of day when most people are fresh; thus they are a good time to deal with questions such as those cited here.

1. Does the diocese where you work have an organization of DRE's?

2. Do you consistently attend the meetings of such an organization?

3. Is your Coordinator group autonomous, initiating its own agendas, or is it dependent on diocesan directives regarding itself and its structure?

4. Have you actively engaged in attempts to bring Coordinators in your area together?

5. Do you and your peers work jointly on programs for consistent and comparable salaries, health benefits, and retirement benefits?

6. Do you have a contract? Is it two-part, between yourself (yourselves) and the parish, or three-part, between DRE, parish and diocese?

7. Do you meet regularly with Coordinators for de-briefing when one or several of you have attended a religious or educational conference?

8. Do you work jointly on programs with other Coordinators?

9. Do you work jointly with DRE's of other denominations than your own?

10. Do you have a procedure for adjudication of disputes and/or firing practices?

4
Managing Organizations

Interest in management and organization procedures has grown among DRE's in the last several years. When the position of DRE first became available, most persons taking it on thought of themselves as in the fields of catechesis or religious education. Administration, management and organization were not of particular concern. For some persons, they even carried a negative connotation, conjuring up the notion of impersonal bureaucracy, rigid authoritarianism, corporate power structures, and cut-throat competition. Gradually, however, the image of those possible aspects of business practice has given way to an understanding that for the work of religion and education to go on, some kind of organization is necessary. It has become apparent that the distinction is not between organization or no organization, but between good and bad organizational practice. In addition, attention to the human side of enterprise in the world of business, sparked by persons such as Douglas McGregor,[1] Peter Drucker,[2] Warren Bennis and Philip Slater,[3] has been widely acclaimed as both enriching and humanizing. Coordinators are beginning to realize there is much to learn from this field that is applicable to their own work.

This chapter is concerned with the relationship between

---

1. See *The Human Side of Enterprise*, New York: McGraw-Hill, 1960.

2. See *The Effective Executive*, New York: Harper and Row, 1968; *Managing for Results*, New York: Harper and Row, 1964; *Management: Tasks, Responsibilities; Practices*, New York: Harper and Row, 1974.

3. See *The Temporary Society*, New York: Harper and Row, 1968.

Coordinators and the organizations most closely connected with their position. After raising questions about three of these relationships, we shall then question the nature of the parish structure itself. Finally, we shall examine the kind of procedures most helpful for Coordinators in their own administrative role in the parishes they serve.

QUESTION 1. *What is the relationship between the Coordinator and the Diocesan Office of Religious Education?*
The question needs to be asked from the other side as well. That is, how does the Diocesan Office of Religious Education see itself related to the Coordinator? Here it might be well to look at diocesan offices as they exist in the United States. There are many ways of structuring diocesan offices, and one can point to a spectrum which includes one-person offices on the one hand to those which are composed of twenty or twenty-five persons on the other. In some cases, all education in the area of religion, including instruction carried on in parochial and diocesan schools as well as the parish, is directed by the diocesan office, acting as a single division. In others, education in the schools is directed by one office (usually the Office of Education, headed by a Superintendent of Schools), while education at parish or deanery level is under the Religious Education Office. In still others, all education in the diocese, whether inside or outside the school, is administered by a single office which has two separate sub-divisions, one for school education, one for non-school education. These divisions are usually referred to as (a) education and religious education; or (b) schools and CCD. The first is semantically peculiar and possibly redundant; the second is indicative of a particularly narrow philosophy of education.

An analysis of the relationship between Education and Religious Education Offices in dioceses where both exist could provide a field day for a systems analyst or fascinating dissertation material for a Ph.D. candidate searching for a topic. In some dioceses, mutual respect, sharing of resources and personnel, and common aims unite the offices in genuine community. In others, an ongoing tension best describes the situation. In still others, power plays and competition for financing and prestige reveal machinations worthy of the Borgias at their best.

As related to the DRE, the Office of Religious Education (we shall arbitrarily stay with that term) carries on one or all of four functions. The first is to act as the arm of the bishop and sometimes as the arm of Rome. Here, the diocesan office sees its major role as explaining and enforcing legislation and directives related to religious or church practice, such as new sacramental rituals. However, the office will also be set up so that diocesan policies concerning textbooks are enforced, parish educational programs are periodically checked, and the credentials of invited speakers at diocesan and parish conferences are automatically reviewed by the chancery. Such a role as episcopal liaison can be double-edged. On the one hand, religious education can flourish where a diocesan staff is able to use its insight and vision as well as its professional expertise in a free and responsible manner. In some dioceses, however, people are shut off from new ideas or scholarly theological discussion by the fiat of a bishop who, often on the basis of rumor, passes the word through the diocesan office that some people, some ideas and some publications are simply not welcome. A Parish Coordinator considering taking on a parish position would do well to investigate first what freedoms and constraints at this level will affect his or her work.

A second role the diocesan office plays is that of supervision, the word being used not so much in its overseer sense as it is to indicate the diocesan office's providing of a "vision beyond" what is now possible, sensing and seeing new directions, and acting as a kind of scouting party for the DRE in exploring new territory. Here the diocesan office might, for example, be engaged in involving marriage encounter couples in education for teenagers, supplying population and age projections for individual parishes that will assist the DRE in planning, setting up experimental or laboratory schools using approaches such as open education techniques in teacher training, and assisting DRE's in understanding the ramification of educational thinking such as Freire's *conscientization*, or Gutierrez's theology of liberation, for the parish situation.

The most common role played by the diocesan office toward the DRE, however, is that of direct service in the day to day work. Many offices are structured so that besides a Director and Associate Director, who more often than not are priests and therefore male, there are staff persons, usually female, for pre-school, elementary, junior high, special education, adolescents, adult education, audio-visual and library, teacher training and sacramental preparation. Since these are ordinarily the areas of concern to DRE's, such staff persons can be of invaluable assistance. They can provide help in knowledge, selection and critique of resources such as textbook series, audio-visuals and bibliography. They can also keep aware of new trends and practices in their respective areas, advising the Coordinator of the better choices to be made and the most appropriate expenditure of funds.

In theory, the most valuable diocesan staff person, although not found everywhere, is someone who is Coordinator of Coordinators. Ideally, this is a diocesan staff person who acts as advocate for DRE's at the diocesan level, especially in such areas as hiring, contract design,[4] securing equitable salary and benefits, and termination of employment. A second role for a diocesan Coordinator of Coordinators is a convening one, where this person assists in bringing Coordinators together to form their own organizations. At this level, the Coordinator of Coordinators can impede creativity by dominating the organization or enhance it by encouraging the organization to become independent in its own structure, policies and procedures, while maintaining cordial mutual relations with the Diocesan Office of Religious Education.

Another function of a diocesan staff is to initiate or conduct programs in individual parishes. The DRE does not always have the resources or the time to do everything necessary in the parish. In such cases, a diocesan staff person might be called on to conduct the teacher training program, a workshop in Parent Effectiveness Training, or a seminar on setting up a parish reli-

---

4. See Joseph Neiman, *Coordinators*, Winona: St. Mary's College Press, 1971, for excellent sample contracts, pp. 30, 35-36.

gious education board. In large dioceses, this may be accomplished by the staff person's working with groups from several parishes. Another option is for the diocesan staff to go into a parish as a unit and operate for several weeks as a diocesan team educating a parish team in the area of concern specific to each person. The DRE needs to be aware of the resources offered by her or his diocesan office and should not hesitate in demanding accountability from staff persons when assistance is needed. Conversely, the DRE would be wise to keep the diocesan office informed of any programs or special area of expertise he or she might be bringing to the parish, so that mutuality might be an expected and ordinary characteristic of the relationship.

The last function of the diocesan office is a modeling one. If the office operates as a community, if it prays and plays together, and if the work of its members is complementary, it provides a powerful model of a miniature church, and even of a parish without walls. One of the most fruitful ways to accomplish this, a procedure copied by many DRE's with their own staffs, is a monthly overnight meeting. When people eat, drink, work and worship together over a twenty-four hour period, when they can debrief the month's activities in leisure and plan for the coming month's activities in relative tranquility away from the interruption of phone calls and the pressure of the immediate task, some possibility exists that the work of the church may be accomplished with care and serenity. To model this for all the parishes in one's diocese may be the greatest contribution a diocesan office ultimately can make.

In the future, all of these functions of the diocesan office may die out. As DRE's become more autonomous and better educated, there will be some question whether any or all of these tasks are necessary. This does not mean, however, that the diocesan office will go out of existence. Instead, as Joseph Neiman once pointed out, it may take on two new functions. The first would be to establish work relationships with other diocesan agencies such as Catholic Charities, CYO, and Research and Development to discover how to work together in areas of mutual concern. For example, the religious education office might develop a program for Catholic Charities staff members where the content is supplied by the latter, but the process conducted by the former. The office might also spend more time with outside agencies at its own level in the political, social and welfare arenas to decide on joint activities. It might also direct its energies to cooperate with the staff offices of other religious denominations in designing ecumenical religious education programs, much as Joint Educational Development is already doing.[5]

The second new task of the diocesan office might be in the area of planning for the future. As Parish Coordinators become responsible, for example, for their own teacher training, diocesan personnel might restructure their time in a way where fifty percent of it would be devoted to tasks at hand and the other half to dreaming for the future and determining how best to help create a new world. Ideally, this is how many of us would like to spend our time; if the diocesan office lives out its modeling function really well, Parish Coordinators may be able to accomplish the same thing themselves.

QUESTION 2. *What is the relationship of the DRE's parish to its surrounding parishes?*

The word is out. Walls between parishes are crumbling and new religious communities are being formed on the basis of criteria other than geography. The phenomenon whereby people in search of vital liturgies cross parish lines in order to sustain their own worship lives has become common. So too has the practice of attending educational programs regularly at parishes other than one's "own." The closing of parochial schools has in some cases cut off the one connection many people formerly had with their parishes. In others it has set in motion all kinds of activities from senior citizen and day care centers to drug rehabilitation programs. Finally, attendance at Sunday Mass by U.S. Catholics, according to some estimates, has dropped as low as fifty percent.

5. See Bettie Currie, "Joint Educational Development: An Ecumenical Endeavor," in *The Living Light*, Vol. 11, No. 4, Winter 1974, pp. 608-612.

These are trends that are easily documented. What is of some importance here, however, is raising the question of how the DRE and her or his individual parish and its personnel will address these trends. There are a number of possibilities, and it might be pointed out here that the most important word in the sentence is possibilities. We are not yet, any of us, in a position to know which way things will go, but we are in a position to identify some of our options and perhaps make intelligent choices before it is too late.

One possibility for all parishes to consider is whether they face a financial crisis. Some parishes are presently receiving more in their collections than ever before; others are operating on shoestring budgets. One reason may be the kind of trends cited above. Another may be the differing socio-economic levels of individual parishes. The question to be raised here is whether parishes with sufficient or more than sufficient funds feel any obligation to share the wealth.[6] Should there be, for example, some central bank to which each member church has access, much on the same basis as do members of religious orders? Do wealthy parishes have responsibilities and obligations to neighboring parishes not as well off? And who decides? On what basis are decisions made?

For example, if a parish maintains a parochial school and ninety percent of every dollar goes to the school, while ten cents goes to all other parish activities, would a neighboring parish be obliged or even justified in sharing financial resources? On the other hand, if a wealthy parish is neighbored by a poorer one in desperate need of housing and health care, can it in conscience close its eyes to such needs?

Here is the first of the serious issues underlying Question 2. If we say we are a church, are we a church of those who are "us," or are we willing to include, in Marie Augusta Neal's phrase, the "non-us-es" as well, in this case, our sisters and

---

6. It might be noted that dioceses have always sought to redress such inequities in the past. The problem on the horizon is different today not only because dioceses themselves face financial troubles, but also because contributors are beginning to demand a voice in the distribution of the money that is theirs.

brothers in poorer parishes? These are issues which lead again to the central areas of sex, power and money. Are decisions on such issues made by men, while women are denied making contributions to decisions? Is power to effect and implement decisions in the hands of one man, a pastor or a bishop, or does the whole community or a representative body of the whole community decide? And if those whose money is being spent decide to withhold that money because they are denied access to decisions about how their money is being spent, what is the future of the individual parish?

Several issues more directly concerning the DRE might also be raised here. The first is whether parishes will decide to share personnel jointly. If one parish cannot afford an adult education director, three or four might be able to share his or her services. Joint educational programs sponsored by and participated in by several parishes would be a similar phenomenon, as would be the presence of resource centers directed by Area DRE's, responsible for the educational policies and programs of a cluster, where there would be joint ownership of materials. All three phenomena tend to blur parish boundaries.

Once this kind of thing happens, the need quickly arises for cooperative planning by the parishes concerned. Needless to say, pockets of parish clusters are already doing this here and there throughout the country. But what is not generally noted in such situations is that this move is breaking down the organization of parishes as we have known them and creating a new kind of unit. When a team of priests, DRE's, school personnel and liturgical coordinators whose people come from several parishes begin planning together, they tend to lose some power in terms of individuality but gain an enormous amount in terms of unity, communal spirit and support. How far this may go is anyone's guess, but DRE's would do well to note its happening, and reflect carefully on the design such a new structure might take.

The other kind of inter-parish programming that may concern the DRE is that which crosses denominational boundaries. Again, this is occurring in many places throughout the country, and it is not an insignificant move. It raises questions of intercommunion and sacramental sharing, of doctrinal differences and similarities, and, at a deeper level, questions of a community's identification as church. Most joint ecumenical programs seem to occur either with reference to social concerns or in the area of religion education, and once again it is suggested that the DRE be aware of the move, reflective concerning it, and cognizant of where it may lead.

QUESTION 3. *What kind of relationship does the DRE share with intra-parish units? Do intra-parish units exist?*

The reference here is to a point cited in passing in chapter two, the move on the part of some parishes to divide the parish into smaller communal units, where all persons know one another, and where size is a critical factor. Sometimes the parish is consciously divided. It may be into family, neighborhood or block units, where several persons are trained as group leaders for discussion, or as directors of sacramental preparation for families in a certain section. It may be as prayer groups which meet to pray and/or celebrate the Eucharist regularly in each other's homes. It may be Marriage Encounter couples who meet together to renew that experience. Or it may be that a team of priests who are co-equals (and not pastor, first, second and third assistant) have each taken responsibility for what are, in effect, mini-parishes within the parish.

Sometimes the division is less consciously made. The natural units formed by the DRE's teaching staff often become genuine communities, like-minded in their reawakened adult interest in religion, and eager to continue study. It is not unusual for the fifth grade teachers, the junior high faculty, or the "home program" participants[7] to become very close in their work together, thus forming many small cells within the larger parish organism. These cells often continue to meet together, even after their work in the religious education program is completed.

---

7. Home program is a term used to describe a program where learners, both children and adults, participate in religious education held in the home of one of the parishioners, rather than in a central building belonging to the parish. Obviously a different kind of environment and dynamic is characteristic of such a program.

Another kind of unit is made up of senior citizens. The problems of night travel coupled with much available free time during the day are natural factors calling senior citizens to meet and study, often the scriptures, at times when most other parishioners are at work or involved in the care of young children.[8]

The DRE is faced with the questions of how best to relate to these units and how to offer to them some kind of continuing education in their religious concerns. Perhaps the most effective procedure is to work with representative members of each unit in such areas as group process, communication, and identification of resources. All of the units used as examples are composed of adults, and adults are quite able to take responsibility for their own education. However, they are often unaware of the wealth of their own resources and not always sure of their own competence. The DRE needs the ability to instill this confidence and point out what resources are available for continuing education. The DRE does not need to convey the impression that he or she is indispensable, for he or she is not.

When such intra-parish units exist, the question of size becomes critical. As has already been remarked, twenty or twenty-five people may be a far more natural parish than ten or twelve thousand, and there is actually no totally convincing reason why it is necessary to keep the meaning of parish solidified as comprising hundreds or thousands. The more scriptural meaning of church is a community of communities, and presently DRE's are in the process of discovering many such communities within their own parishes. It then becomes a choice whether to encourage the life of these communities as autonomous, although related to the larger group, or to put the large group first with an oblique but intentional criticism that the smaller units are somehow schismatic.

It is in such situations that the question of sacramental celebration once again becomes paramount. With senior citizens and home-bound parishioners, extraordinary ministers are al-

---

8. Recently, in a talk at the New Orleans Catechetical and Pastoral Institute, Msgr. Wilfred Paradis commented that if current birth rates continue in the U.S., half the population will be over 62 by the year 2000. DRE's would do well to note this trend.

ready acting as Eucharistic ministers through the service of
bringing Communion, and this ministry appears bound to become more extensive as smaller communities grow in their own
identity. It appears to be leading toward a time when the extraordinary minister will act in the capacity of penance cele-
brant as well (a quiet Catholic question already surfacing), and
where the community will begin to address on serious scriptural
and theological grounds its own role, responsibility and activity
in the celebration of the Lord's Supper.

QUESTION 4. *Is the parish organizational theory X, Y, or
other?*

In 1960, Douglas McGregor coined the terms Theory X
and Theory Y to explain two differing and opposing views of
human nature as they related to work.[9] A Theory X Organization is basically autocratic and authoritarian, based on the belief that people dislike work, need firm orders, and expect and
appreciate decision making by others above them. Theory X
makes wide use of rewards and punishments, believing them
necessary to oil the organizational apparatus, is characterized
by a secrecy where people are given only that information necessary for their own activity, and is predicated on the assumption that there is necessity for tight control from on top.

In contrast, Theory Y organizations are participative and
communal. They are based on the belief that when given a
choice, people prefer to work and to make contributions. In this
model, human beings are encouraged to make decisions at their
own level. They also have wide access to information in a climate of openness and sharing. Rather than motivate through
rewards and punishment, the Theory Y assumption is that once a
person's bodily (food, clothing, shelter) and identity (Who am I?)
needs are answered, their work within an organization is mo-
tivated by a concern for society, exemplified in the asking of
Bonhoeffer's question "How is the next generation to live?"
with its corollary "And how can I help?"

It is not too difficult to transfer these theories to parish

---

9. McGregor, *op. cit.*

structure and to realize that they and the psychology underlying them are operating in parish life as well as in business. To take one example, the sanctions of rewards and punishment (heaven and hell) have been greatly undermined as a basis for moral activity by the theological climate following Vatican II. The need to take responsibility for one's own decisions and their consequences is seen more and more clearly, especially by the young, as is a genuine distrust of decisions made by others without consultation of those involved in the decision. Religious questions are asked of and considered answerable by all in the community and not solely by someone officially educated and ordained for that purpose. Finally, the creation of parish councils, finance and education committees has given a voice to a once silent majority of parishioners, and one man's veto becomes less and less powerful without the support of the parish community.

DRE's would do well to assess their own parishes in terms of their organization along X or Y lines. Such an assessment will determine whether DRE's have the pre-conditions necessary to execute the programs and objectives they see as vital to their parish community. The best way to begin such an assessment would be by a consideration of their own presuppositions concerning human nature and whether their own attitudes are X or Y. This might be done by asking a close friend, one's spouse, or one's immediate community to reflect back to them whether their insights about themselves are correct. If they are considering a position but have not yet been employed, their interview of clergy and parish board ought to include questions in this vein. Finally, it is important to assess the general attitudes of parishioners in the given situation. As pointed out in our section on change agents, parish members themselves differ in their attitudes toward renewal, and it is not at all uncommon for parish "leaders" to be closer to Theory Y than other parishioners.

Once such consideration is accomplished, there is need to add the "other" dimension. It is to be remembered that the theories considered above were developed in business, and business is geared toward production and marketability of products. Parishes, in contrast, at least ideally, are religious communities which come together to celebrate their belief in a transcendent Other, to better the religious qualities of human lives, to search together in covenant with one another through the puzzles and ambiguities of life, and to live out the command in Isaiah 58:6-9:

> Is not this the sort of fast that pleases me
> —it is the Lord Yahweh who speaks—
> to break unjust fetters and undo the thongs of the yoke,
> to let the oppressed go free
> and break every yoke,
> to share your bread with the hungry
> and shelter the homeless poor,
> to clothe the one you see to be naked
> and not turn from your own kin?
> Then will your light shine like the dawn
> and your wound be quickly healed over.
> Your integrity will go before you
> and the glory of Yahweh behind you.
> Cry, and Yahweh will answer;
> call, and he will say, "I am here."

No theory will accomplish these objectives; they are ultimately dependent on the people's faith, hope, charity and prayer, and, most of all, on the presence of the Spirit in their midst.

QUESTION 5. *Has the Parish Coordinator learned to set goals and objectives?*

For someone who works in a parish and is responsible for programs and planning as part of an administrative role, the ability to clearly design goals and objectives is an invaluable skill. Goals and objectives have for a long time been part of educational planning although there is some question of their appropriateness in learning theory. Here, however, we are looking at goals and objectives organizationally with reference to the planning of programs.[10] The distinction to be made is that while

---

10. Probably the best known handbook for setting goals is Robert F. Mager, *Goal Analysis*, Belmont: Fearon, 1972. See also his *Preparing Instructional Objectives*, Belmont: Fearon, 1962.

persons as learners may set off in one direction that initially is clearly designed, and then decide to follow a path that appears only tangentially, thus arriving at a goal or objective that is totally different from the one planned, a *program* is more helpful if it is clearly and specifically described, and observable, measurable outcomes are set up as indicators of whether the goal has in any way been achieved.

The word Goal is the answer to the question "What do I want to do?" and the word Objectives is the answer to the question "How do I know it is being done?"[11] Goals are abstract, overall and comprehensive; objectives are concrete, observable and measurable. Examples of goals in a parish situation might be:

1. To develop a program for teenagers in the area of social concerns;

2. To form a pastoral team directed to the education of adults;

3. To set up a liturgical committee responsible for the creation of styles of worship appropriate for various participants;

4. To design a sacramental program of penance preparation, involving children and their parents.

The reader is invited to notice the language appropriate to the articulation of a goal. Phrases such as "to develop," "to form," "to set up" and "to design" are helpful as starters. However, there is nothing in the language of the goal to answer the question "How do I know it is being done?" This is the function of objectives, which are designed to put the goal into operation. To take the first example above, for instance, how would a DRE know if she or he were in fact developing a program for teenagers in the area of social concerns? What would

11. For this language I am indebted to Dr. Joanmarie Smith, Chairperson of the Department of Philosophy at St. Joseph's College, Brooklyn, New York.

be actual activities that are observable and measurable in practice, spelled out not only in terms of actual days and hours, but hopefully having target dates as well? Some might be:

1. To convene a group of ten parish teens on Tuesday, September 7, from 7 to 10 p.m. to focus on five areas of social need in the parish.

2. Consideration of busing, unemployment, drug use, the elderly and housing as possible areas of study.

3. Identification of three resources (books, persons, agencies which would be named) which can supply information concerning these needs.

4. Developing from the group of ten persons, five teams of two people each who will be responsible for surveying or interviewing the resources cited.

5. Report on their survey by the ten teens due on Tuesday, September 21, from 7 to 10 p.m.

6. Selection of one or two areas for extended study.

7. Follow-up meeting on Tuesday, September 28, to set up a program of activities.

Notice, all of the above are part of the *development* of the program. At this point a new goal is emerging, which might be stated: "To plan definite activities for a teen program directed to social concerns." Moving on to observable, measurable activities, the objectives might read:

1. To interview five people who are elderly, or unemployed, or in need of adequate housing, to determine their assessment of their own situation.

2. Interviews will include such questions as: "What would you like done that would assist you with this problem?" A sample response from an elderly person might identify a need for the parish to develop meals-on-wheels

programs (a goal) or a service by young people doing shopping and errands for senior citizens (objectives).

3. Listing of needs and possible actions teens could carry out, based on the interviews.

4. Study of legislation, legal penalties and sanctions in the particular area of concern. Example: What are the penalties locally and state-wide for drug use?

5. Spend one entire day with a person on welfare, or at court on a drug charge, or in a senior citizen home, to experience the situation from the inside.

The list is endless in possibilities. The point is, however, that as programmers for the parish organization, Coordinators need to develop skill in designing goals and objectives if they are to be competent in the managerial tasks assigned to them. They cannot be so without extended practice, not only in designing goals and objectives with care and specificity, but in the task of putting them into action to insure that they are carried out.

STRATEGY NO. 7: ASSESS YOUR DIOCESAN OFFICE

The following strategies are models for the processes of assessing and designing goals both individually and collectively.

1. Does the diocesan office dictate the programs to be used in your parish and are sanctions applied if their directives are not followed?

2. Does the diocesan office periodically bring to your attention new educational and theological trends? Does it suggest pilot and/or experimental programs to you?

3. Does the diocesan office assist you in the development of your programs through staff persons? Can you name the staff persons and their area of responsibility?

4. Does the diocesan office periodically publish a newsletter listing new materials helpful to you in your work?

5. Do Coordinators have an advocate in the office who is especially concerned with the DRE?

6. Have you ever called on the diocesan office staff to conduct programs in your parish?

7. Does the diocesan office provide a model of community?

8. Does the diocesan office work closely with other diocesan agencies, and, if so, does this affect your parish in any way?

9. Does the diocesan office work with other social, religious and educational groups at its own level, and, if so, does this affect your parish in any way?

10. If you could redesign the diocesan office to meet your needs more adequately, what would this design be like?

11. Do you keep the diocesan office informed of your activities, particularly in areas of new programming, so that these might be available to other DRE's?

12. Does the diocesan office maintain resources you use in the line of books, manuals, films, etc.?

13. Do you feel any responsibility to your diocesan office?

14. How do you demonstrate your feeling of responsibility to the diocesan office?

15. Will you submit your responses to these questions to your diocesan office?

STRATEGY NO. 8: OVERNIGHT STAFF MEETING

The following is a design for an overnight staff meeting to be used either by a DRE or a diocesan staff. You are invited to fill in or revise the design, or perhaps use some of the strategies suggested in this book.

FRIDAY - (THURSDAY):

3:00 p.m.	Meet at ⎯⎯⎯⎯⎯⎯ Retreat House.
3 - 5 p.m.	Debrief previous month's activities via each staff member's comments on his or her own previously submitted, outlined report.
5 - 5:30 p.m.	Break: free time; prayer.
5:30 - 6:00 p.m.	Pre-dinner refreshments.
6:00 - 7:30 p.m.	Dinner and free time.
7:30 - 9:00 p.m.	New business. Setting goals and objectives *or* Input from invited guest *or* Film *or* Presentation by one staff member *or* . . .

SATURDAY - (FRIDAY):

8:00 a.m.	Breakfast
9:00 a.m.	New business. Design one's own format.
10:15 a.m.	Break
10:30 a.m.	Resume meeting
12:00 noon	Liturgy
12:45 p.m.	Lunch
1:30 - 3:00 p.m.	Closing: e.g., film; art forming; new media display; conclude business; closing prayer.

STRATEGY NO. 9: DEVELOPING GOALS AND OBJECTIVES

For the following goal, develop at least ten specific, observable, measurable objectives:

Goal: To set up a liturgical committee responsible for the creation of styles of worship appropriate for various participants.

Objectives: 1.

2.

3.

4.

5.

6.

7.

8.

9.

10.

STRATEGY NO. 10: DEVELOPING GOALS AND OBJECTIVES

For the following goal, develop at least ten specific, observable, measurable objectives.

Goal: To form a pastoral team directed to the education
               of adults.

Objectives: 1.

               2.

               3.

               4.

               5.

               6.

               7.

               8.

               9.

              10.

STRATEGY NO. 11: DEVELOPING GOALS AND OBJECTIVES

For the following goal, develop at least ten specific, observable, measurable objectives.

Goal: To design a sacramental program of penance preparation, involving children and their parents.

Objectives: 1.

2.

3.

4.

5.

6.

7.

8.

9.

10.

STRATEGY NO. 12: PROFESSIONAL AND PERSONAL GOALS FOR THE DRE

Cite one way in which your presence, *professionally*, has made a difference in the parish in the past year.

Cite one way in which your presence, *personally*, has made a difference in the parish in the past year.

State, in focused terms, one goal you hope to achieve professionally by January 1. Draw on the experience cited above, and include measurable objectives.

State, in focused terms, one goal you hope to achieve personally by January 1. Draw on the experience cited above, and include measurable objectives.

5
Managing Time

Very few problems at the practical level engage Coordinators as constantly as the management of their time. The manifold duties they are called on to perform, the necessity to conduct evening sessions during the week, the programs that must be held on Saturdays and Sundays, and the overnight staff or retreat meetings that form part of their continuing agenda can push them toward an all work and no play mentality that is often inhuman, sometimes frustrating, and potentially damaging to them personally. The expectations laid on them by others and sometimes their own super-demands on themselves quickly become problematical unless DRE's can carefully analyze their own attitudes toward time and the inner resources they bring toward handling it. Such an analysis is the purpose of this chapter, and the questions posed here are intended as a means to achieve it.

QUESTION 1. *What distinction does the DRE make between inner and outer time?*
Undoubtedly, this is the most important time question to be raised. Most of our notions of time are directed toward outer or clock time, the exact amount of hours and minutes available to us to accomplish particular tasks. This amount of time never varies; no matter how much we hurry, we still find ourselves with only twenty-four hours each day. What is not always noted, however, is that we do possess an inner kind of time, characterized not by the passage of minutes, but by the quality of the present in which we live, and by the intensity of awareness we bring to this present. We experience inner time when we remark about a completed experience, "That time just flew," or

"I thought that would never end." In these two cases, the amount of outer time may be exactly the same. The quality and intensity of our awareness of it, however, is so different that we find the nature of the time itself is different. This is the experience of inner time, and the first step toward time management for the DRE is toward enlarging this experience.

Deepening our awareness of inner time is not to be thought of as a technical gimmick geared to produce extra work. As westerners we are already far too prone to produce and to get things done. On the contrary, growth in understanding of inner time is intended to humanize us, to integrate us, and to help us achieve serenity and tranquility in the ongoing present. It is intended to stretch us inside, to give us psychological space, and to slacken the frenetic pace at which many of us find we live our lives.

How do DRE's develop their sense of inner time? The first and most important component of this development is probably the nature of their prayer lives. Prayer itself can be looked upon as one more thing to get done; here, however, I am suggesting it as time specifically devoted to the opposite: toward one's doing nothing at all, toward achieving nothing at all, but simply toward be-ing in the presence of the Holy. Some Coordinators enjoy such a style of prayer and guard it jealously. Others had the ability to pray at one time but seem to have lost it. Still others are searching to achieve it but have not as yet discovered a "way."

Here is one instance where our own society can be of great help to us. Part of the problem for most people in our culture has been the collapse of "plausibility structures,"[1] frames of reference where a particular world view shapes our activity. For religious and church people, the collapse of a supernatural world view, and often of a childish and set notion of God, has deprived them not only of a context in which to pray, but also of a sense of Whom to pray to. What many in our society have discovered in this situation is a new mode of being, of praying,

1. See Peter Berger, *The Sacred Canopy*, New York: Doubleday Anchor Hook, 1967, pp. 45-48.

and of stillness. One example is interest in transcendental meditation, Zen and the practices of Yoga. Another is participation in Mind Control, which is to some degree a combination of these three, but, even more, a practice which begins with progressive relaxation, and often leads to deepened awareness and to freedom from the outer constraint so harmful to prayer. A third is the simple Gestalt technique of sitting down quietly, closing one's eyes and sharpening one's sensitivity by completing the phrase "Here and now I am aware of . . ." in as many ways as possible.[2] A fourth is the setting aside of one day a month, or one hour a day, where one finds a quiet and hidden place, and brings only oneself and a book—scripture, poetry or a story—or some music—Bach, Beethoven or jazz—and in that context simply waits upon God. Some people are fortunate enough to carry this solitude with them all the time; most of us need to consciously provide the discipline and environment ourselves. But all of us need the experience of tapping the inner time within us, and the more this becomes an aspect of part of every day, the more it becomes possible for it to be the undersong for all of each day.

QUESTION 2. *Does the DRE periodically keep a time log?*

The keeping of a time log is one of the most practical procedures one can engage in to manage outer time. As the phrase suggests, a time log is a record of where one's time actually goes, and not an agenda for where one will plan to spend it. Peter Drucker comments in *The Effective Executive* that one of his first questions to busy people intent on managing their time is to ask them to tell him how they spend it.[3] He writes down their initial responses and then directs them to keep a precise and detailed record for the next several weeks, day by day, hour by hour, and minute by minute, to assess where the time actually goes. What Drucker has discovered, and what parish personnel often find, is a wide discrepancy between where people think

---

2. See Everett Shostrom, *Man the Manipulator*, New York: Abingdon, 1967, pp. 66-67.

3. *Op. cit.*, p. 27.

they spend their time, and where they spend it in reality. For example, we may think we spend ten minutes each morning at a coffee break, and discover by keeping a time log that it is more like thirty. Or we may think of a meeting as taking two hours of time, but realize that travel before and after the meeting plus time spent in answering individual questions informally has extended the actual meeting time to four or five hours. We may think we devote an hour each morning to professional reading, but discover that actually the books remain half read on our shelves. Keeping a time log, at least one or two days a month, is the first step for DRE's in finding out where their time actually goes.

QUESTION 3. *How does the DRE decide on priorities for the spending of time?*

Once one has a sense of where the time actually goes, the next step is to carefully assess the different activities listed in the log as A, B, C, Cz or Cd. Next to the activities listed in one's time log, persons can learn to prioritize them by noting whether they are A activities, essential and important; B activities, of less importance, or C activities, of minimal importance.[4] Coordinators find, as most people do, that they spend too much time on C activities and do not set aside enough time to accomplish A activities, those high priority tasks that are the ones ultimately of most importance in the overall picture. One reason is that A activities are generally more difficult, demand more psychic energy and often involve confrontations or potential conflict with other people. They are the ones for which we generally have to do a great deal of personal "tooling up." The way we tend to tool up, however, is by doing a great many C activities, C's being ones that are relatively easy and productive of a great deal of immediate satisfaction. Most of us, for example,

---

4. See Alan Lakein, *How To Get Control of Your Time and Your Life*, New York: Peter Wyden, 1973. This, and Drucker's *The Effective Executive*, Robert Townsend's *Up the Organization* and James McCay's *The Management of Time*, Englewood Cliffs: Prentice-Hall. 1959, are among the more helpful works on procedures to deal with time management.

are quite adept at the C activities of rearranging the books on our shelves in alphabetical order, straightening out our closets or bureau drawers, counting the number of pens and pencils we have currently usable, sharpening the pencils and testing out the ball points, and rereading papers on our desks or moving them from one position to another. We do the last, for example, even though we are quite aware of what is in the papers, and conscious that the actual task is answering them if they are letters, editing or rewriting if they are newsletters, and taking a proposed action if they are requests.

Dealing with the C's however, can lead us to the A's. Lakein suggests that we subdivide C's into Cz's, things that really do not need doing at all and which if left aside long enough can be thrown away, and Cd's, delegable activities that someone else is willing and able to do. A great many Cd's fill the time of DRE's, especially when they come to their second and third year in a parish. By this time, they know the people they are working with, their strengths, capacities and availability, and can easily pick out those things they did the first year that can now be handled by someone else. Resistance to sharing such tasks may indicate a certain authoritarianism at times, a reluctance to ask for assistance at others, and unresolved guilt problems in a third, especially if the delegation means one will have more leisure time. Cutting down one's working week from sixty to forty or forty-five hours would be a luxury for most people; DRE's who feel guilty[5] when they have less to do than usual perhaps need some self-examination in the reasons why they feel this way.

Once one has a sense of the A's that need doing, one has acquired the ability to identify priorities. The final problem becomes how to get ourselves to actually do them. One way is to set a target date (for people who "work well under pressure"). Another is to write a list of things to do tomorrow, as one finishes at one's office, perhaps taking the last fifteen minutes of the day to do so. On the next day, a wise procedure is to

---

5. Peter Barnett, a DRE from Bay Shore, New York, refers to them as "workaholics."

go through the list, noting whether proposed actions are A's, B's or C's. Generally, on a list of ten activities, two or three will stand out as of major importance, and if possible these should be done first, particularly if one has morning time available, since 9-11 a.m. is for many people their most productive and refreshed period. The B's can be done later, and, ideally, the C's not at all. Eventually, the DRE will discover that doing the most important things immediately and well has enhanced the quality of her or his professional activity, as well as the results of this activity.

QUESTION 4. *Has the DRE learned the nature and conduct of meetings?*

We have already noted in passing the great amount of time DRE's tend to devote on each day or every other day to meetings. Probably no other activity takes as much of the Parish Coordinator's time on a year-in, year-out basis. It would seem, then, to be of some help to consider in detail the nature of meetings, the most effective procedures for holding them, and the most important problems involved in their conduct as well as ways of dealing with these problems.[6]

There is a verse of Rudyard Kipling's particularly helpful for all planning, but especially appropriate in a consideration of meetings:

I have six honest serving men;
They taught me all I knew;
Their names are how and what and when
And where and why and who.

These six are questions to be reflected upon prior to every meeting, although the arrangement here is slightly different: *why* is the meeting being held, *who* is to be involved, *where* will it be

---

6. For assistance in integrating this material on meetings, I am again indebted to Dr. Joanmarie Smith.

held, *when* will it occur, *when* begin, *when* end, *what* materials are needed, and *how* best proceed during the meeting.[7]

At the outset, it might be remarked that some management consultants have suggested that meetings are marks of poor organization. Ideally, many meetings need not be held. Therefore, the initial question to be asked is why we are holding a proposed meeting, and whether the goal in mind might be as easily achieved by some other procedure. Unless there is a specific goal to be achieved in holding the meeting, it should not be called. It is not just a nuisance to have an unnecessary meeting, it is a danger to community to hold an unnecessary one. Most people are aware of belonging to organizations where there is a dreaded monthly meeting, dreaded because the only reason for the meeting is a decision somewhere along the line to hold a meeting regularly. A better solution for such organizations might be to ask members to hold a certain day open, the second Tuesday, for example, in case there is some reason to meet.

Generally, there are four major reasons why DRE's hold meetings.[8] The first is for purposes of information. If this is the stated purpose, then the first consideration ought to be whether a meeting must be held to gather it. Could the information to be shared be mailed, or disseminated in some other way? If information is to be collected, could it be mailed or phoned in to the persons seeking it? Often, information meetings are the most unnecessary, and one would do well to cross off one's list any planned solely for this purpose.

A second reason for holding meetings is for purposes of clarification. Here, one must ask whether clarification is indeed called for on some issue, and, if the answer is yes, how the organizer of the meeting knows that it is needed. Further, how many persons need clarification? Does everyone invited to the

---

7. For the Kipling quote and the questions, I am indebted to the work of James Schaefer. See his *Program Planning for Adult Christian Education*, New York: Newman Press, 1972.

8. Excluded in this section are teachers' "meetings" which are educational in nature and actually learning sessions. These will be considered in chapter eight.

meeting need to be there? We may discover that in actuality only two or three persons are in this position, and they could easily be reached by a phone call. Thus one must again ask if this is a good enough reason to hold a meeting. If the answer is still affirmative, clarification itself must be seen as an art. The person originally making the presentation that has called for clarification should rarely if ever be the one called on to clarify, and if confusion is still evident, the slow process of having the parties repeat points raised by others *to the satisfaction of those others* should be engaged in.

A third reason meetings are held is covert. That is, the actual purpose of the meeting is social, geared toward helping participants become a closer unit or toward getting to know one another better. However, business meetings are often held to accomplish this social purpose. The caution to be mentioned is that one ought not have a business meeting if the real reason is social. Instead, one should do something else: arrange to demonstrate the conduct of a new educational process, have a picnic or show a film followed by discussion, design a liturgy or prayer service, or celebrate the contributions of members through a party.

Generally, the best and most appropriate reason for holding a meeting is to make a decision. Prior to announcing the meeting, however, it must be asked whether on the one hand the decision is big enough or inclusive enough to warrant a meeting —for example, the selection of a fourth year textbook—and, on the other, whether the decision is too comprehensive to be made by those involved at the meeting. With reference to the first, Theory Y organizational practice dictates that such decisions be made at another level, by those using the textbook, teachers and students. With reference to the second, the decision might be too large for the group involved—for example, to stop the formal teaching of religion to children. It may be that a recommendation decided on and passed along to a larger decision making body is called for in such an instance. One must also be wary of decisions that cannot possibly be implemented because the diocese, parish at large, or pastor will block implementation. In such cases, recommendation may be the wiser course and in the long run be the quickest and most politically astute move in insuring eventual implementation.

Included in the question of holding a meeting, once it has been decided upon, is the preparation involved where those invited have all the information necessary beforehand in terms of minutes, committee reports and planned agenda. An opening question at meetings, in order to insure participants' familiarity with the proposed business, would then be to ask whether they have read the information sent prior to the meeting as well as whether there are prior questions of clarification before the actual business begins.

The second major aspect of a meeting is the choice of participants. For whom is the meeting necessary? Who is to be invited? Is it a workable number of persons, and how are they to be informed of the meeting? Is the attendance of certain resource persons necessary, and should officers of parish committees be invited as observers? Is the presence of the pastor or clergy important for the morale of participants? Not everyone first considered needs to be present, and one procedure for the DRE would be to send a note saying, "I have asked Mary, Theresa, Betty and Joe to attend a meeting on the topic of _____. Please come if you need information or want to take part in the discussion. In any case, you will receive a summary of the meeting with a request for your comments." This can save DRE's much time in conducting meetings, alert them to those which appear unnecessary, and keep the number at a workable size. In the beginning, some persons may still feel obliged to be present, but if the DRE creates a sharing climate, those who do not necessarily need to be present will feel free to pass up a meeting.

Another consideration here is whether everyone who needs to attend can indeed come, or whether it is necessary to change the proposed time. The problem of baby sitters is a major one that is not always taken into consideration by DRE's, especially if they do not have families themselves. The problem of sitters is one that the DRE might take in hand, in conjunction with the teen-age program, for example, with an awareness of the actual cost in money to the participants if baby sitters are needed. For meetings held during the day at the parish, baby sitters should be provided as a matter of course.

The third major element in planning for a meeting is consideration of the physical environment where it is to be held. The nature of the surroundings can have a major effect on a meeting, and rooms with rugs are to be preferred to those without them, soft lights to harsh ones, and comfortable and adequate seating to cramped quarters. Ventilation is also important, as are bathroom facilities and access to a phone. A table where participants can sit in a circle facing one another is particularly helpful, and if the DRE makes sure that there are pencils and pads of paper available for participants waiting at their places when they arrive, a sense of importance and seriousness is communicated even before the meeting begins.

Time is a more difficult element to arrange than place. The day and time of any meeting is usually selected as a compromise, where there is an attempt to reconcile the note of efficiency, that is, the time of day when people are most alert and energetic, with expediency, that is, the only time people have available, which may be after work, after Mass, after class or on a weekday morning. Of critical importance too is the practice of starting and ending exactly on time. If a meeting is scheduled for 8:00 p.m., it should begin then even if only two participants are present. Many people are chronically late for parish meetings, not because it is impossible to be there on time, but because experience has taught them that 8:00 p.m. really means 8:20. Similarly, if participants know they will end promptly, even if business is not finished, those meetings which must be held will be attended and participated in with far greater involvement than those that tend to drag on as a matter of course. Body time is important too; if the DRE senses that people are too tired to arrive at consensus, it would be a better choice to adjourn and to meet again, rather than arrive at agreement by exhaustion, where the uppermost consideration in participants' minds is pushing something through in order to conclude an overlong meeting. The former is, again, more consonant with Theory Y organization. Finally, as Phil White points out, there are some ethnic groups that do not operate with the same time rhythm characteristic of much of the society. This too needs to be taken into account, and adjustments made accordingly.

The most important aspect of the "what" of a meeting is its agenda. Beforehand, all participants should be advised as a matter of course of the proposed agenda, with the opportunity to add to it whatever is pertinent. The agenda itself should be mailed to each person beforehand, with a proposed time allotted for each item. Duplicates of the agenda should be saved for the meeting itself, to insure that everyone present has a copy. It may not always be possible to remain with the proposed time stated on the agenda, but often Parkinson's Law is very much in evidence at meetings: work does expand, or contract, to fill the time allotted for it.

Finally, the how of running a meeting is very much up to the leader. Many of the leader's functions have already been described in chapter three. It might be added here that the role of a chairperson is fourfold: to see that the meeting begins and ends on time; to see that the meeting keeps moving; to see that no one dominates and everyone is given a chance to speak; to see that the objectives of the meeting are achieved. For larger meetings, Robert's Rules of Order might be considered a helpful procedure. What is of paramount importance for chairpersons, however, is that they move the meeting by questions and avoid declarative sentences entirely. This can be done by asking questions such as: "Shall we begin (close, move on to the next point)?" "Would someone else address this point?" "Would you tell us, Betty, your thinking on this point?" (to someone who has not spoken). "Are we content that such and such has been decided?" If the chairperson wants to talk in declarative sentences, it is better for her or him to ask someone else to run the meeting, a situation that may be handled by revolving the chairperson role, or asking for a volunteer once the job description for a particular meeting is understood.

As for voting on a particular issue, the rule is to *strive* for consensus and only *resort* to majority vote when this fails. The caution to be observed here is that everyone must be able to live with decisions made at a meeting. If this is not possible, dissenters have the responsibility and obligation to keep up their dissent; otherwise attempts at implementation may be foiled. When and if stalemates do occur, discernment techniques might be used, where time and prayer are directed to "pros" and "cons" of an issue. Argument itself is, of course, an art, as opposed to getting something off one's chest or making an announcement. For genuine argument, one must listen objectively, repeat points to the other's satisfaction, attempt to keep feelings of threat, anxiety, worry and enthusiasm from interfering, beware of using and/or reacting to "tune-out" words and labels, and avoid being a naive helper who fails to recognize a genuine argument by stating "You two are really saying the same thing" when this is not actually true. Participants, but especially the chairperson, must avoid their own hidden agendas as far as possible, refrain from interpreting others' experience for them, and accept what people are saying at face value if they want to move the meeting, genuinely persuade others to their point of view, and arrive as far as possible at the best decision. It is important not only to make it as psychologically easy as possible for others to change their opinions, but to be prepared as well to change one's own if new light indicates that is the direction in which to move.

Finally, with respect to future meetings, it is always of some assistance to provide some evaluative instrument which will allow participants to reflect on past meetings and make whatever changes appear necessary. A checklist with opportunity for comments can be distributed at the end of the meeting, with time provided for participants to return it immediately. If this is not feasible, then stamped self-addressed envelopes for participants to mail their responses back to the DRE are well worth the investment. The objective, it is to be remembered, is the management of time, and input from the widest number of people is one of the most helpful devices for insuring that time is well, and not poorly, spent.

STRATEGY NO. 13: KEEPING A TIME LOG

For three consecutive days, list the activities you actually do, recording them as they happen. Divide the half hour periods into ten or fifteen minute segments where necessary.

7:00 a.m.	3:30 p.m.
7:30 a.m.	4:00 p.m.
8:00 a.m.	4:30 p.m.
8:30 a.m.	5:00 p.m.
9:00 a.m.	5:30 p.m.
9:30 a.m.	6:00 p.m.
10:00 a.m.	6:30 p.m.
10:30 a.m.	7:00 p.m.
11:00 a.m.	7:30 p.m.
11:30 a.m.	8:00 p.m.
12:00 noon	8:30 p.m.
12:30 p.m.	9:00 p.m.
1:00 p.m.	9:30 p.m.
1:30 p.m.	10:00 p.m.
2:00 p.m.	10:30 p.m.
2:30 p.m.	11:00 p.m.
3:00 p.m.	11:30 p.m.

STRATEGY NO. 14: PRACTICE IN SETTING PRIORITIES

Below are listed fifteen typical activities of a DRE. Label those you feel are:
—of primary importance A
—of secondary importance B
—of minimal importance C
—which need not be done Cz
—which are delegable Cd

1. Write memo to pastor and parish council describing last night's parent meeting.

2. Send memo to pastor and parish council.

3. Meet with third grade teachers to plan tomorrow's lesson.

4. Call bus company to arrange for senior citizens' outing.

5. Set up room for meeting of primary grade mothers.

6. Pick up filmstrip for tomorrow's parent meeting from diocesan office.

7. Eat lunch.

8. Have snow tires changed on car.

9. Continue reading Silberman's *Open Classroom Reader.*

10. Attend lecture on "Morality and Youth."

11. Cash check at the bank.

12. Review new pamphlet series as possibility for adult education discussion group.

13. Have toothache checked by dentist.

14. Pray.

15. Take data from parents of children preparing for Eucharist.

STRATEGY NO. 15: SETTING ASIDE TIME FOR TOP PRIORITIES

1. On the first of each month, circle a day during the following month when you will find a quiet, hidden place and spend the day in prayer.

2. On Sunday morning, look at the week ahead and pick out an hour each day for professional reading.

3. On Sunday morning, look at the week ahead and pick out an hour each day to be spent in prayer and/or solitude.

4. On Sunday evening, look at the week ahead and decide which two days during the coming week you will take off *in succession.*

5. On Monday morning, look at the week ahead and schedule an hour a day at your office when there will be no interruptions. Incoming phone calls will be returned after the hour is over.

6. On Monday morning, look at the week ahead and schedule an hour for lunch on at least *two* days.

STRATEGY NO. 16: PLANNING FORM FOR MEETINGS

1. Why is this meeting being held? Information, clarification, social, decision making, or other?

2. Who needs to be involved? How and when will they be contacted?

3. Where will the meeting be held?

4. When will the meeting be held? On what day? At what time will it begin? At what time will it end?

5. What materials will it be necessary for you to have before the meeting?

6. What evaluation procedures will be provided to assess the meeting?

STRATEGY NO. 17: CHECKLIST FOR MEETINGS

Remote Planning Check:

Schedule day, time and place for meeting.
Notify participants, giving travel directions or diagram for new members.
Notify those whose participation is welcome, though not necessary.
Send agenda to participants no later than one week previous to meeting, to give time for additions. Include stamped, self-addressed envelope.
Receive revised agendas, if any, from participants.
Send revised agenda to participants.
Certify that new participants have been invited to come with participants familiar with the procedures.
Keep second copies of agenda available for meeting itself.

Immediate Check:

At least an hour prior to meeting, see that chairs and tables are set up.
Check that chairperson has pre-visualized the meeting.
Check that paper and pencils are provided at each place.
Provide copies of minutes, agenda, reading material (if needed) at each place.
Have timer, clock visible when time limits have to be set.
Check light, ventilation, ash trays, cleanliness of bathrooms and whether they have sufficient soap, towels and toilet paper.
If equipment is to be used, check to see that it is in working order.

Actual Check:

Begin on time.
Move meeting by questions.
Make sure each participant speaks.
End at stated time, unless obvious consensus to move on ·

Make sure extension time, if any, extends no more than 30 min-
    utes.
Set date, time, place for next meeting, if needed.
End on time.

Post Check:

Solicit evaluation verbally through reflection on key points, atti-
    tudes toward decisions made.
Solicit evaluation in writing through yes or no check of:
    Was this meeting necessary?
    Why or why not?

6
Managing Managers?

The title of this chapter is posed as a question to indicate the disparity between this and the two previous chapters. One can learn to manage an organization, one can learn to manage time. But people are generally not to be managed; they are to be loved, hoped in, believed in. The word "generally" is used here to indicate that manage in the sense of controlling, bringing about by contrivance, or keeping someone submissive is inappropriate in human relationships, although manage may take on the positive meanings in "direct" and "guide" as well as the ambiguity in the term "husband." Nevertheless, the answer to the question posed in the title "*managing* managers?" is, generally, "No."

The managers referred to in this chapter are all those persons who work with the DRE in some kind of directing, guiding or administrative parish role. The focus of this chapter will be on the identification of such persons, the kinds of attitudes most likely to build relationships between them and DRE's, and some of the relevant issues for Coordinators to consider in their own managerial roles.

QUESTION 1. *Has the DRE the ability to identify the key people in the parish?*

In order of priority, after praying, the first things DRE's would be wise to do when entering a parish is to ask: "Who are the key persons here?" The question may be phrased in a number of ways, each with its own nuance. For example, the DRE might ask: "Where is the power here?" "Whose influence is critical in developing programs?" "Who will be allies and who must be allies if I am to accomplish anything?" "Where and from whom am I likely to find resistance?" "Are there any small communities within the parish with whom I might work?"

Identifying the key persons will vary in different situations. Someone who is a parishioner already may know the answers to the above questions even before he or she begins the task of DRE. Coordinators new to a parish, however, would do well to ask of everyone they meet: "Is there anyone you can suggest that it is important for me to know?" and "Is there anyone to whom it is important I talk?" The responses will tend to fall into three major areas, and Coordinators will need to keep these three in mind if they are to be effective managers in the parish.

The first group of people are those who are obviously in positions of parish power. Many of them will be daily co-workers of the DRE. These are usually people who participate in the process of interviewing the DRE prior to hiring. Thus it will be important to establish rapport with such persons from the beginning, to listen sympathetically to their vision of the parish, and to communicate with them as peers on the professional level. The pastor is almost always, at least at this time, *the* key person for the Coordinator. He is the chief administrator in the parish, its liaison with the diocese, the keeper of the funds and the liturgical leader. His say can often, if not always, make or break a program. Before accepting a position in any parish then, it is very helpful for the prospective Coordinator to get a genuine sense of the pastor's style and assess carefully whether they will be able to work together. Often, especially if the Coordinator is a woman and the first Coordinator to be employed in a parish, the pastor will be experiencing, for the first time in his ordained life, a co-worker engaged in the same pastoral activity as himself who is of equal or almost equal status in the parish, and of equal or superior education. Coordinators would do well to be sensitive to the threat this poses for some pastors, to tread lightly and gently for both human and political reasons, and to keep the pastor informed from the very beginning, by memo or personal contact, of what they are doing. Coordinators in the role several years have pointed out that often their initial years might have been marked by far less friction if only they had been wise enough to keep open communication between themselves and the pastor.[1]

In a similar role to the pastor is the principal of the parochial school, if a school exists in the parish. Often the school building is used for many parish functions, but there seems to be a venerable Catholic tradition, operative in many places, which assumes that if anything is broken, marred or defaced in this building, it is the fault of those who come for "religious instruction." There is also a possibility that when a program in religious education outside the school exists and is successful, it poses a threat to the parochial school. Finally, the obvious fact almost everywhere is that a parochial school takes a great percentage of financial resources from a parish, but operates for only a small group of parishioners. All of these factors make the presence of the DRE a genuine threat to the parochial school's viability and the embodiment of reaction to this threat is often the school principal, whose attitude in such cases may range from non-involvement and non-awareness to actual coldness.

Certainly, this is not always the case. Many Coordinators enjoy fine mutual personal and professional relationships with principals, where there is sharing of resources and programs, and where the DRE is coordinator of the religion program in the school as well as throughout the parish. When this occurs, the Coordinator discovers, as many already have, that the parochial school faculty can be enlisted as resource persons to assist volunteer teachers, that books, audio-visuals, equipment and ideas can be shared, that sacramental preparation and initiation can be jointly developed, and that the scandal of a divided parish community need not exist. One key to avoiding this scandal is to work at building a strong relationship between the principal and the DRE.

Of tremendous importance to the Coordinator will be

---

1. See Joseph Neiman, *Coordinators. op. cit.*, for an excellent discussion of the question, in chapter four, "Working with the Pastor," pp. 79-106.

parish clergy other than the pastor, or, where the clergy are a genuine team, simply "the priests of the parish." Prior to the hiring of DRE's, Catholic church practice in the U.S. has been to assign the program in religious education to one of the parish priests who became "Moderator of the CCD." Seminary training has not generally prepared priests well, if at all, for this role, but this situation appears to be changing throughout the country, in many cases with remarkably positive results. One has only to visit some of the year-long or summer programs in religious education and/or pastoral ministry throughout the country to meet many priests of all ages who are responsible for innovative and adult-centered religious education in their own parishes. Such men are usually pursuing degrees which complement their seminary preparation, or updating their professional understanding of religion and education. They and their brothers in the parishes are often a source of great support and encouragement to DRE's, and almost always, when interested and involved, are his or her strongest allies.

Of growing importance in recent years have been parish council members who often have voice and vote in parochial concerns. In some cases, the DRE is ex officio a member of the parish council; in other cases this is not true, and the decision in this matter seems best determined in the individual situation. However, in all parishes where there is an operating council, it is imperative that the DRE be involved as representative of the parish educational interests, and as catalyst for the entire parish community's commitment to its educational role. Many times, a parish education committee exists as an agent of the parish council and is responsible for the design and implementation of educational possibilities, especially for adults. When such education committees exist, they and the DRE can be mutual resources for one another; when they do not, the DRE might consider establishing such a committee after a year or two in the parish. Here again is an instance where the diocesan office can be of assistance to the DRE, instructing him or her in the administrative procedures for establishing parish education committees.

A second kind of key person in every parish is someone in

the role of "informal" leader. These are people who might be characterized as Communicators, who have high visibility and who are influential in molding opinion. DRE's need to identify these informal leaders and to enlist their assistance. They will be found everywhere: the sister in the convent who has taught generations of first graders, the mother of nine who has always been a volunteer in parish activities, the coach of the parish CYO team, the rectory housekeeper, the parents of the young man who said his first Mass years ago in the church, the school secretary. To each of these, the DRE should candidly address the questions: "What is it important for me to know and do?" and "Will you help me to do it?"

Finally, there are key persons in the parish who are relatively powerless in one sense, but tremendously powerful in another. These are those who are acknowledged as representatives of the young, the old, the poor, the unschooled, and racial and ethnic minorities. Each of these groups has its leaders and its spokespersons. Some have been disenchanted by the church, rightly or wrongly, and have become suspicious of concern when it is manifested by someone in an official church capacity. At other times, notably in parishes of the central cities, the poor and the oppressed, the young and the old, have created vital, dynamic communities that draw on the multiple and varied resources of their differing Christian traditions as well as the services of city or county agencies. The Coordinator who wishes to encourage religious community will need much time to build up trust among such persons when it is lacking. But where trust exists, these are the persons among whom the DRE's efforts can bear the greatest fruit, from whom the DRE can learn the most, and without whom the parish can never be a genuine community.

QUESTION 2. *Does the Coordinator take time in building a bond of trust?*

In the development of any human relationship, time is a major factor. A saying exists in religious orders even today that one needs to live with someone four seasons to truly know him or her, to which the wise have added the corrective, "No, five."

At any rate the point to be made for Coordinators is the necessity for giving all their relationships within the parish time to mature, to do very little at first in the parish besides studying it, and to involve themselves in many situations in the parish, playing many roles. For the truth is that while they are observing other parish members, DRE's are in turn being observed—a normal, human process. When parish functions are held or groups within the parish engage in some activity—a play perhaps—the DRE can do more by bodily presence at such activities than by giving a month of Sunday homilies about religious education, although this last suggestion need not be automatically excluded. However, the main contribution a DRE can make toward creating a bond of trust is to do the job for which he or she was hired. Listening to others, sharing their lives, presence, and hard work are noticeable qualities, and where DRE's involve themselves in parish life with obvious concern, they are contributing in the best possible way toward the creation of a bond of trust.

QUESTION 3. *Does the DRE identify and organize strengths, rather than deal with weaknesses?*

If there were one principle a Coordinator could use in working with others in parish managerial roles, it well might be: feed strengths and starve weaknesses. DRE's need to know the talents, interests, gifts and expertise of those with whom they work. It is these, their strengths, which can be used to benefit the parish; little good is accomplished by focusing on what is lacking. Thus a key managerial task becomes the identification of specific abilities of co-workers, and the movement with this grain rather than against it.

One can begin to assess others' strengths by informal conversation. DRE's can inquire what books their co-workers read, what their families are like, what their hobbies are, how they spend their spare time. Most importantly, they can search out past achievements, looking for the kinds of situations in which other parish managers have not only *been* successful, but *felt* successful, especially when there has been some kind of public acknowledgment of the achievement. The principle underlying this search is positive motivation. If a person has been able to accomplish a task satisfactorily, he or she is more likely to be moved to repeat it. The opposite is also true. Where one has never succeeded, where one has not been moved to try, or when one has had a negative experience, there may be a sense of learning something; nevertheless, one generally remarks about such experiences, "I would never want to do that again."

Besides informal conversation, the Coordinator can discover strengths by structured activities. Workshops in positive motivation often begin with sessions where teams of people share their two-minute autobiographies with one another, and then go on to list five or ten achievements in their lives of which they are proud.[2] This kind of sharing allows co-workers to see each other in positive guise, and rarely, if ever, appears gimmicky, stilted or discomforting. Rather, it provides a systematic approach that allows people to focus specifically on the accomplishments of each other. For example, one may discover musical talent by hearing that a co-worker conducted a children's choir for years; facility with numbers upon hearing of math contests won in high school; perseverance in a fifty-year-old who decided to return to high school; love for the sick in a hospital volunteer, as well as bilingual, secretarial and reflective skills. It goes without saying that all of these are strengths valuable to a community.

Once strengths are identified, the next step is to organize them. The Coordinator looks at a planned program and then asks: "What strengths in my co-workers can I call upon here?" One DRE enlisted eight Dominican sisters in her parish school to do grade level training of teachers once a month. Another called on her pastor, a former scripture professor, to speak to adults on the New Testament. Another enlisted a lawyer and a bank manager in the parish to help, respectively, with housing questions and the best use of meager funds in purchasing equipment. Another enlisted a bilingual parishioner to translate all

2. For one of the finest positive motivation sessions in this country, see James J. Nugent, *Achieving Individualized Motivation Systems*, PMA Institute, Inc., Village of Poquott, 37 Van Brunt Manor Road, Long Island, N.Y. 11733.

written communications into Spanish. Culinary experts have been called on to suggest menus, artists to share knowledge of crafts, and carpenters to build bookshelves, carrels and chairs for learning centers. Elementary and high school students have been called to work with younger children or peers on a one-to-one basis where groups have been too large or where the children have been apparently disinterested due to an impersonal learning climate. In all cases, the stress is on what people can do and enjoy doing, and no member of the parish is too young or too old to be excluded from contributing if he or she wishes to. Such can only happen, of course, when DRE's know their people; hence the importance of genuine alertness to the gifts of co-workers.

A second approach to identifying and organizing strengths is to brainstorm together, with other parish managers, the strong points of the parish itself. One may discover positive qualities such as the parish geography, presence of ethnic groups with distinct sub-cultures, commitment to social concerns, and political astuteness. Each facet of parish life may be similarly analyzed. Has there been any attempt by the parish to set up cooperative food or clothing operations? What are positive accomplishments of the parish council and where might they lead? What has been done by and with youth groups? How has music in the parish been a contribution? In what ways has the administration of the parish been responsive to parishioners? What are the circumstances that have resulted in appropriate liturgies and how might these be repeated? Where have the poor been assisted? What neighborhood agencies are resources?

The point of asking these and similar questions is to arrive at a realization of the good points already in existence, and the utilization of these as a springboard for future action. What is usually discovered, when such positive brainstorming occurs and a moratorium declared on negative feedback, is the enormous good already present in every situation, the possibility of more of the same, and a feeling of pride that a community possesses the ability to move toward realization of its ideals.

QUESTION 4. *Is the Coordinator's managerial role accu-*

*rately defined and are the pre-conditions for such a role spelled
out in detail?*

Throughout this book, the allusion has been made to the
necessity for accurate job descriptions for DRE's, and to the almost certain over-extension entailed by the position itself. A difference exists between the kinds of duties a Coordinator fulfills
the first year and the changes which occur in the role as he or
she begins a second, third or fourth year in the same parish. As
one gets to know the people and the situation, as one becomes
part of a religious education community, there is almost always
a change in emphasis; old duties are delegated and new ones un-
dertaken. Therefore, it is generally wise to let a job description
be in effect for just one year, particularly the first. The changes
from first to second year are major. The first year, a Coordinator often feels like someone in a boat continually plugging
leaks. He or she rushes to plug the leak, does so, and sits back
only to find that another leak has sprung. The second and third
years, one begins to build, to foster small interactive communities, and to establish continuity with what has gone before. As
the years go by, changes in the role are far less noticeable.
though they may, paradoxically, be far more innovative.

It is a function of the Diocesan Office of Religious Education to provide general job descriptions. The circumstances in
individual parishes are so different, however, that it is not likely
that these will completely fit. Therefore, it is to the novice
Coordinator's advantage, when she or he is interviewed, to ask
for a description of role expectation in as great detail as possible, in the three areas of administration, education and religion,
with a built-in understanding that adjustments will be necessary
at the end of each year. For persons seeking several job descriptions by way of comparison, two sources are the National Conference of Diocesan Directors, based at the United States Catholic Conference in Washington, and the Parish Coordinator
Sub-committee of the Religious Education Association.

Mutual understanding on the part of parish and DRE must
exist during the hiring process. Those doing the hiring need to
be as clear as possible prior to interviewing candidates about
what they wish the person to do. At the same time, the prospec-

tive Coordinator needs to be as transparently honest as possible
in envisioning how much he or she is able to do. Both parties
need to be aware that changes in the role are to be expected.
However, if a new task is to be assigned after hiring, it should
first be presented to the Coordinator; if a task is taken on by default or by necessity by a new Coordinator, this too should be
made known. There is no substitute for candor and communication, and it should take place as soon as realization of a change in
task has occurred.

This leads to the question of contracts. Besides defining the
role of the DRE, a contract should make clear who the hiring
party is, to whom the DRE is responsible, what rules, if any,
apply to the expiration or termination of contract, and what
health, retirement, insurance and travel benefits, if any, are
included. It is not unknown for Coordinators, with or without
contracts, to be fired at whim and told to leave in the middle of
a contract period. It is also not unknown for DRE's to contract
for a position and then fail to carry out their part of the agreement. Contracts need to address these problems, and most
DRE's are well advised to seek legal counsel before signing a
contract.

The question of salary is definitely problematical. One of
the major elements of the problem is the discrepancy of salaries
for Coordinators from diocese to diocese; in some places Coordinators are considered as professionals, must possess a Master's degree, receive cost of living increases as a matter of
course, and are considered on a par with such ten-month employees as high school teachers. In such dioceses, starting salaries for someone with no experience may be $9500 or $10,000,
with $15,000 or $16,000 the salary for someone with graduate
degree(s) and years of experience. To make up for the differences
in vacation time between school personnel and DRE's, dioceses
grant funds for continuing study in some cases; others assume
the position is a ten-month one, and the summer is free as a
matter of course. In contrast, other dioceses have no set salary
policy and individuals are left to negotiate as best they can with
very little comparative information as backup, and no advisory
agency to consult. It would seem that Coordinator Associations

in individual areas are the best agents to deal with these questions. That, however, raises another, perhaps even more delicate problem.

I refer here to the discrepancy in benefits and salaries that tend to exist for lay men and women on the one hand, and for members of religious orders on the other. Men and women not in religious orders are often envisioned as costing a parish far more than sisters, brothers or priests, and salary differentials may appear to be several thousand dollars. This obviously places a question of financial strain directly before a parish. Several questions, however, need to be addressed as this issue arises.

The first is whether the church in general wishes the role of Parish Coordinator to be one held exclusively by men and women in religious orders, or whether a sense of community will involve men and women, single, married, or belonging to orders, in this role of co-official. The financial question is part of the situation, but opening the role on a major scale almost certainly gets at the deeper problem of whether power will be shared across the board by all church members. At this time, many married men and women are DRE's, but it remains an ongoing problem, particularly when there are children to support, whether this work, which most of the married DRE's see as positive, humanly fulfilling and personally important, is one they can afford to continue. Young, single women face a problem that is somewhat different. As in most businesses, the question often rises in an employer's mind whether the single woman is a risk because it is assumed she will eventually leave the job to marry, become pregnant, and decide to raise a family, rather than continue working. Thus, equal employment and affirmative action policies need to be part of parish situations as they are in the wider society.

Another underlying question is whether the assumed discrepancy actually exists. Non-members of religious orders pay federal, state and city taxes, religious order members do not; the former pay rent and car installments where sisters and brothers most often do not (although this is changing) or are given a car to use. Retirement and health benefits are usually minimal for the former when given; for the latter these security problems have not surfaced as yet as a major question although they seem bound to do so as the median age in religious orders keeps rising. The power to be brought toward dealing with these issues lies with those in religious orders more than with their brothers and sisters outside, and thus it is imperative that they come to understand the problems in justice being raised here. They also need to address the question that will almost surely be theirs in the next ten years of having to pay taxes as do all other citizens. In the meantime, however, they face the very real question of whether they are doing themselves and the wider church a disservice by continuing to accept as salary far less than they are worth. The most obvious and easiest solution would appear to be that all Coordinators in a diocese be placed on the same salary scale, dependent on educational background and experience. This would remove the double standard now operating in such situations, and would leave members of religious orders free to turn back whatever they wish to the parish as "contributed services." This is a policy familiar to religious orders which operate colleges, where salaries on the books are the same for priests, brothers and nuns as they are for all other faculty, but where the actual remuneration allows religious order personnel to turn back much of their salary.

Coordinator Associations throughout the country have tended to address these issues recently with more and more seriousness. The critical question, however, will continue to be whether the issue is seen as one concerning only some of the DRE's, or whether it will be understood as the problem of all— to be shared, addressed and solved by a united Community of Coordinators.

QUESTION 5. *What is the managerial role of the Coordinator toward his or her teachers?*

No persons in the parish are as immediately the DRE's concern as the persons who form the religious education teaching staff. They are the managers of the religious education program at every level and are those most closely involved with the Coordinator. When they have been teaching in the parish for years prior to the hiring of a DRE, they may have one of three attitudes. The first is support and assistance, which is invaluable for a new DRE in getting a sense of what has happened before, and providing continuity and a feeling of acceptance. The second is where the presence of a DRE suggests to teachers that their responsibility is now over; someone has been engaged full time on a financial basis to do that for which they had been volunteers. This attitude often, but not always, results in such persons leaving the staff, but with the positive evaluation that things are in competent hands and their own work is completed. A third attitude is more difficult to accept; it is one that sees the Coordinator as an outsider or interloper, and results in little or no cooperation, whether the persons decide to stay on or to leave the program. Generally, whatever the attitudes of former teachers, first-year Coordinators find themselves in a position where there is a major shift in their teaching personnel, if for no other reason than the initiation of new programs which entail more people. Thus the managerial role of the Coordinator tends to be fourfold: selection of teachers, definition of relationships, guidance and termination.

Informal surveys and interviews with Parish Coordinators indicate that there is little uniformity throughout the country in the processes for selecting and hiring teachers. Presuppositions are widely different, as is the language used to speak of personnel, and this may contribute to the absence of consensus. For example, some Coordinators feel that people involved in an educational role in the parish are persons engaged by a call, who are ministers of the Word and part of a task that is spoken of as pastoral ministry. Thus, their personnel are not teachers, but catechists, and their objective is participation in and understanding of a revealed Word, directed toward the formation and establishment of a "faith community."

In contrast, many Coordinators see their primary area as education, rather than catechesis. They seek to engage men and women with religious commitment who have an understanding of educational philosophy, styles of teaching and pedagogical method, and whose skills are in the areas of communication, learning theory and group process. This tension between either pastoral ministry or education as the underlying basis for teacher selection is a serious one and will be returned to in our next chapter. It does, however, affect the fourfold managerial role of the DRE in selection, definition, guidance and termination. Selection of personnel is accomplished in numerous ways. Announcements from the pulpit or in the parish bulletin may draw many who wish to participate in the church's educational mission. Personal contact is another vehicle, and here most DRE's acknowledge that time taken to visit the homes of prospective teachers is more effective than the somewhat impersonal phone call. The former gives both DRE and prospective teacher an opportunity to assess the situation and the other person and indicates a seriousness and concern not communicable across the wires. A third procedure is an appeal for assistance after Sunday Masses where the Coordinator meets people outside the church in an informal manner and notes names of interested persons as well as suggestions of faculty from those who stop to inquire. None of these procedures, however, indicate that there are pre-set criteria, and the Coordinator might do well to reflect with other parish personnel whether there are certain characteristics, expertise and experiences pre-requisite in a person invited to teach, as well as whether a poor teacher is better than none. It might be helpful, for example, to solicit responses from interested persons as to why they want to teach, what their understanding of teacher-student relationships might be, whether they *like* children, teens or other adults, as the case may be, and what resources they feel they would bring to the parish educational program.[3] Ideally, they might be invited to join the program much as student teachers do, that is, as assigned to a master teacher responsible for breaking them in. John Dewey made a suggestion similar to this years ago. Remarking on the benefits to education of a master-apprentice situation, Dewey had complained:

---

3. For a significant approach to teacher competency, see "The Role of the Teacher in the Church," *Instroteach, Inc.*, P.O. Box 2314, Wichita, Kansas 67201.

. . . beneficial consequences extend only to those pupils who have personal contact with gifted teachers. . . . The only way by which we can prevent such waste in the future is by methods which enable us to make an analysis of what the gifted teacher does intuitively, so that something accruing from his work can be communicated to others.[4]

DRE's would most certainly be well advised to ponder this notion.

What must be avoided, however, is a situation where anyone who is signed up to teach is automatically accepted without any prior instruction or initiating process where he or she is apprised of expectations. This is both unprofessional and unfair. A better procedure is a preliminary set of introductory seminars where people can examine the role as defined and feel free to decline it, while the Coordinator works with them as assessor of their possibilities and either confirms them in the role or offers other options such as audio-visual consultants, teaching aides, pastoral assistants (persons engaged in other parish activities such as sacramental programs and home visiting) or administrative assistants. Teaching is not the only role for which persons are needed.

Once prospective teachers are selected, however, defining relationships becomes a primary responsibility for the DRE. Several expectations must be communicated in this defining process. One is whether the basis of participation will be voluntary, which carries with it some possibility of minimal involvement, or remunerative, where participants know they are taken seriously because they are paid, even if it is a nominal sum. Remuneration can, of course, take a number of forms: several subscriptions to religious education journals are automatically sent to teachers; weekly or bi-weekly courses are offered to them as a support in their ongoing task; grade level meetings are held periodically to analyze feedback and problems and to

---

4. In *The Sources of a Science of Education*, New York: Liveright, 1929, pp. 10-11.

suggest innovative and proven procedures; baby-sitting is a service provided or paid for by the parish, and fees for diocesan or regional courses and conferences are taken care of as a matter of course. On a more human level, Coordinators need to set up periodic teacher (or catechist) appreciation celebrations where it is very clear that there is an acknowledgment of the ongoing contributions of their personnel. (Some DRE's begin the year with an initiatory rite or celebration where teachers are officially "commissioned.") One corrective: no one should be selected simply because a body is needed; if there are not enough teachers, prospective students would benefit more by being placed on a waiting list until competent persons are available; liturgical celebrations can be looked on as participative communal experiences where religious learning, though unplanned, is a beneficial side effect; and periodic youth retreats or day long gatherings where the educational structure is different from formal instruction might be suggested as alternatives. In the long run, such activities may prove even more beneficial to students in coming to a realization of the religious dimension of their lives.

Guidance of teachers is the Coordinator's third managerial task. One aspect of this is to super-intend, that is, to look together with teachers at their intentions in working with any group of students. Whether it is with ten first-graders in a home program, or with college students in a study of busing, the teacher can be guided in his or her work to reflect aloud on aims, hopes and possible outcomes with the DRE, or with other parish personnel who are on the DRE's team. In conjunction with the teacher's reflection, the DRE must also allow for reflection on the part of students. Major problems in teaching tend to occur when the teacher's perception of what is happening is totally different from the perceptions of those who are her or his students. The DRE needs to be aware of the perceptions on each side of the relationship and to bring incongruent perceptions to the attention of both parties.[5] A second aspect of guidance to be offered by Coordinators is the exhibition and ex-

5. For assistance in this delicate procedure, see Thomas Gordon, *Teacher Effectiveness Training*, New York: Peter Wyden, 1974.

planation of areas of student interest which may escape the new teacher's notice. Younger students in the cognitive stage of concrete operations will, of course, be most involved when working with actual materials; older students will tend to grapple with provocative ideas, once their thought processes have become developed. This entails some knowledge of cognitive, psychological and religious development of students on the part of the DRE, since such background is invaluable in assisting teachers who may be expecting either too little or too much because they are unfamiliar with their new role.[6] Here it may be important to encourage teachers, particularly when they are parents, to trust their own judgment in going with a class even if it seems to be far away from the topic at hand. Years of parenting gives many people a sense of what is important to those younger than they are, and if they intuitively pick up that a group needs to move in a particular way, they should feel free to do so. As Dwayne Huebner once remarked, too much attention to "covering material" may end up as precisely that: covering (up) the material, and hiding it from view. A last aspect of guidance important to the Coordinator is the provision of information to teachers. This may entail either the Coordinator's periodic visits to a teacher's group or a planned session where teacher and DRE can reflect together on the substance of what is being taught. It is not unheard of for teachers, even today, to be providing misinformation to students (confession is necessary prior to the reception of the Eucharist); hence the Coordinator must set up sessions where clarification, correction and input are available to those in need of it.

The last and most difficult of the Coordinator's tasks, as it is for any manager, is the termination of position for someone who is incompetent or inadequate for the work. It is a role demanding refined sensitivity, it is almost always avoided until the last possible moment, and it is rarely pleasant. Nevertheless, there are situations at the professional level where one must tell a co-worker that her or his skills are not adequate to the task

6. See Gabriel Moran, *Design for Religion*, New York: Herder and Herder, 1970, especially chapters five and six.

under consideration. Such a communication should always be preceded by preliminary conversations. It should never be based on rumor or undocumented assumptions, nor should it be an occasion for resolving personality differences. Ideally, the decision to terminate should be offered to the persons themselves, to be made as gracefully as possible under the circumstances. Returning to the principle of identifying and organizing strengths, the DRE should strive to have several alternative possibilities open for anyone in this predicament and do everything possible to cushion what is for most people a painful experience. Prayer and patience are requisite here; it is a time when the DRE must invoke the Holy Spirit:

> Wash the stained soul,
> Water the parched,
> Heal the wounded.

> Make supple the rigid,
> Warm the cold,
> Straighten the crooked.

Being asked to resign, or being fired is a time when one must depend on other resources besides oneself. It is only when the genuine prayer is

> Give to your faithful
> Who trust in you
> Your sevenfold gift

that the pain of termination can be healed, and the Spirit will respond to the prayer that concludes:

> Give reward to goodness,
> Give salvation at the end.
> Give joy everlasting. Amen. Alleluia.

STRATEGY NO. 18: ORGANIZING STRENGTHS

1. Describe a project that the parish will undertake during the year under your direction.

   Description:

   Goal:

   Objectives:
   1.

   2.

   3.

2. What strengths will you call on in the planning of this project?

   1. Of your own:

   2. Of colleagues:

   3. Of the parish as a whole:

STRATEGY NO. 19: IDENTIFYING REPRESENTA-
TIVES OF KEY GROUPS

List one or two people you have discovered to be key representatives of the following groups in the parish:

Young:

Old:

Poor:

Unschooled:

Racial leaders:

Ethnic leaders:

Other:

STRATEGY NO. 20: IDENTIFYING STRENGTHS IN THE PARISH

List five accomplishments of the parish as a whole in the past year:

1.
2.
3.
4.
5.

List five accomplishments of the parish council during the past year:

1.
2.
3.
4.
5.

List five accomplishments of the parish religious education program during the past year:

1.
2.
3.
4.
5.

List five accomplishments of the parish youth (senior citizens, etc.) during the past year:

1.

2.

3.

4.

5.

N.B. Two rules for this strategy are: (a) no negative comments are allowed; (b) there is no limit on the number of aspects of parish life about which the above questions might be asked.

**STRATEGY NO. 21: , PERSONAL CHECKLIST
FOR DRE PRIOR TO
ACCEPTING A POSITION**

1. Has an accurate and detailed job description been provided?

2. Are the number of hours the Coordinator is to work spelled out as clearly as possible? Is there provision for two consecutive days off weekly?

3. Is there provision for a yearly change in this job description?

4. Is it clear to the DRE who the hiring party is?

5. Is it clear and acceptable to both DRE and hiring party what rules, if any, apply to expiration or termination of contract?

6. Is there to be a contract?

7. Are health benefits provided for the DRE as for all other diocesan employees?

8. Is the DRE free to choose his or her own insurance agency, or is it mandatory to accept the one chosen by the diocese?

9. What retirement benefits, if any, are offered?

10. What provision, if any, is made for cost of living increases?

11. Is there any car allowance? Gas allowance?

12. Is there any allowance for travel connected with educational conferences?

13. Is there provision for continuing education?

14. Is there legal counsel available to the prospective DRE prior to the signing of contract?

15. Is there a yearly vacation? How long is it? When may it be taken?

STRATEGY NO. 22: TEACHER SELECTION

The following questions may be answered individually, but would prove more valuable as the agenda for a Coordinator Association meeting. The answers might help to achieve uniformity and professionalism in the selection, ongoing guidance and termination of teacher activity.

1. Cite at least three procedures you have used in the selection of teachers.

   1.

   2.

   3.

2. Cite at least three characteristics or qualities you look for when selecting teachers.

   1.

   2.

   3.

3. What are some of the questions you ask of prospective teachers in an interview?

   1.

   2.

   3.

4. On what grounds would you decide not to select a person as a teacher in your parish program?

1.

2.

3.

5. What are at least three procedures you use for the ongoing education of your teachers?

1.

2.

3.

6. Have you any suggestions for other DRE's concerning the termination of a teacher's role?

7
Education: The Overall Framework

The second major area of the Coordinator's work is educational and will be the concern of this and the two following chapters. Consideration will be given here first to the basic framework from which parish educational activity grows. This issue underlies the more personal attitudes toward teaching which will be discussed in chapter eight, and some alternative educational frameworks open to DRE's today, which will be considered in chapter nine. Here, however, we shall focus on the foundational questions which support the work, the criteria or valuing processes aiding reflection upon it, and the way the Coordinator views the future of religious education as a direction in which to move. We shall also raise the question of freedom as central to religious education, and, finally, make some comments on the nature of adult-centeredness.

QUESTION 1. *Out of what basic religious education framework does the Coordinator operate?*

At the end of Chapter 6, in commenting on the selection of teachers, it was noted that Coordinators appear to operate from different frameworks in considering religious education. The purpose of Question 1 is to lift these frameworks to the level of serious reflection and to indicate the ramifications of each.

The first framework is that which sees activity as stemming from the base of education. Here it is possible to design a pattern where each aspect of education stems from a wider base that supports it, and where each aspect can fit into the larger framework. A diagram of this framework would look like this:

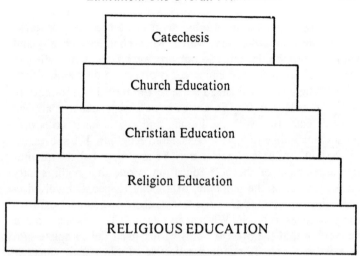

Here, the base is called religious education, and the term is to be reflected upon with semantic precision. The noun is education, and it is modified by the adjective religious. I use the term here as Whitehead does in *The Aims of Education*, when commenting on education as a general cultural activity.

We can be content with no less than the old summary of educational ideal which has been current at any time from the dawn of our civilization. The essence of education is that it be religious.

Pray, what is religious education? A religious education is an education which inculcates duty and reverence. Duty arises from our potential control over the course of events. Where attainable knowledge could have changed the issue, ignorance has the guilt of vice. And the foundation of reverence is this perception, that the present holds within itself the complete sum of existence, backwards and forwards, that whole amplitude of time which is eternity.[1]

---

1. Alfred North Whitehead, *The Aims of Education*, New York: Macmillan, 1929, p. 23.

In this view, the term religious may be used as a criterion for all educational activity, which, when conducted ideally and without coercion, intimidation or propagandizing, and with reverential concern for the educatee, is deserving of the qualification, "religious." Whitehead's use of the term is a reminder to church people that they do not own the phrase, but that all who work at education with the human and professional skills they possess may hope to have it considered religious. The substance, or content, or subject matter may be anything, but the qualitative assessment of the best education is one that realizes duty and reverence as the outcome. Many church people involved in education understand that the test of their own educational activity is measurable in Whitehead's terms. They work from a perception that the present holds within itself the complete sum of existence, seen from the perspective of Christianity in their case, yet containing the whole amplitude of time, which is eternity. Such an ideal of education is also supportive of the more focused and second activity, "religion education."

The term religion education, as used here, is synonomous with such terms as religious studies or the objective study of religion. It has to do with an educational activity where the content or discipline being studied is the phenomenon of religion, seen generically, or, for example, through the perspectives of sociology, anthropology, psychology, literature or art. In such study, although the religious commitment of the teacher may be of the strongest kind, the sharing of this commitment is not part of the instructional intent, nor is the student's coming to a specific religious position a behavioral objective. The intent may be conversion, but the conversion intended is one based on intelligence and understanding where the individual may make her or his own choices. The agent is not proselytizing or proclaiming, but instructing; the material is not presented with claims to certitude but with phenomenological discipline. Again, religion education may be carried on by church members, but it is in no way restricted to them as their special province.

Christian education is somewhat narrower than religion education in that the specific content is understanding, practices and formulation of perceptions of reality as seen from the perspective of one religion or of one religious group. In this case, it might be best thought of as a sub-division of religion education. However, Christian education can take on a number of other meanings. It may be education conducted by Christians, although addressing many other content areas besides religion.[2] Catholic education, which at this point in history still appears to mean education conducted in schools run by Catholics, would be one example. Other examples of Christian education might be educational programs run by Christians in such areas as housing practices, legal rights for oppressed people, or bilingual instruction for persons without facility in English. It might be noted here that in Protestantism most religion education is spoken of as Christian education.

It is here that some overlap with the next aspect of religious education, church education, becomes most apparent. The distinction between Christian and church education as they are being presented here is that the first is not necessarily connected with Christianity in its institutional form. Once the church itself becomes the agent, one is probably more accurate in describing the activity as church education. However, church education is almost always characterized by the fact that those being educated are church members and bring to the educational situation either a predisposition toward church membership or actual membership in the church as baptized persons. Presuppositions of personal acceptance and commitment to Christianity are operative here, and the content becomes more focused on one's membership in a Christian church, one's responsibility toward it, and one's going out to the world with a sense of care based on one's Christian belief and understanding.

In Roman Catholicism, the particular activity of education within the church, for and by church members, with concentration on scripture, tradition, and active church membership, is catechesis. The first draft of the National Catechetical Directo-

2. See Gabriel Moran, *Vision and Tactics*, New York: Herder and Herder, 1968, p. 15.

ry defines catechesis as "the efforts of ministers of God's Word to bring the Catholic people to a mature and lively faith."[3] The problematical aspects of this definition, particularly in view of the distinctions being made here, are obvious in the paragraph containing the definition. The document does not make what would appear to be important and necessary distinctions, but reads instead:

> In this document, the expressions "catechesis" and "religious education" are used interchangeably. They refer to the efforts of ministers of God's Word to bring the Catholic people to a mature and lively faith. The synonomous use of these terms is done as a convenience here until such time as there is a clearer preference for one or the other—or perhaps another more suitable expression.[4]

The problem arising here is the subtle yet undeniably narrow assumption that religious education is owned by the Catholic Church. Hopefully, no educator wishes to be guilty of such an assumption, since it would place her or him in an untenably triumphalistic position. Most people who describe themselves as catechists would want to claim the positive meanings in church education, Christian education, religion education and religious education as their own, and there is no theoretical reason why they may not do so. This will remain a difficulty, however, until church educators, and DRE's in particular, become conscious of the misuse of language that occurs in the equation of the terms religious education and catechesis. Semantics, it is to be remembered, is an exact science that deals with the meanings of words. Semantically, catechesis and religious education do not have the same meaning, and one way out of continuing the misuse of them synonomously would appear to be a careful attention to

---

3. See the "National Catechetical Directory for Catholics of the United States," first draft, Washington: National Conference of Catholic Bishops, 1975, p. 6.
    4. *Ibid.*

the way we speak of our educational work.[5] Another option is new terminology. In *Design for Religion*, Gabriel Moran attempted the move toward what the Directory suggests, the coining of another more suitable expression, based on redefinition of the field of religious education, which he called "ecumenical education."[6] Unfortunately, Moran's attempt has not as yet been picked up.

The ambiguity that results from the blurring of the terms religious education and catechesis has caused some church education people to suggest as a base for catechesis not religious education, but pastoral ministry. This is the second framework that Coordinators, sensitive to the problem of language, have chosen to adopt.

Instead of education as the basic framework, the underlying foundation for educational activity is described as pastoral ministry. Here, in reflecting on the church's mission, persons will note that there is, in the church, a ministry of the Word, a ministry of reconciliation, and a sacramental ministry. Within the ministry of the Word, there is instruction and participation in mature and lively faith, where the ministers of God's Word seek to articulate religious faith as experienced by Christian people, and to carry on both an informing and a forming role. Obviously, this is a consistent and comprehensive framework, but it is far narrower than the framework of education. In addition, it raises several ecclesiastical and political problems.

The first is whether the narrower framework reflects the world situation. Is religious education as carried on in the church reflective of an ecclesiocentric world view in an age where the church is obviously not the center of the universe? Is God's Word something that belongs only to the Catholic Church, or is the Word of God unconstrained, and discoverable

---

5. One might use as an analogy the efforts of many writers and teachers today to speak of the "human" rather than "man" or of "men and women" or "her and his" in referring to human beings. Such efforts have had the effect of changing perceptions through changing language.

6. *Op. cit.*

everywhere? Is revelation "a universal phenomenon, present in the life of every individual and of all religions"[7] with a corresponding Christian interpretation of this universal revelation? Or is revelation preserved in one institution which is the custodian of God's Word, constraining and confining it definitively?

Undoubtedly, most DRE's would not make this latter superior claim today, but the point that is being made here is that catechesis does indicate in its definition that God's Word is found in one central institution. Still another problem occurs when speaking of catechesis as a "forming" role. Is forming another person's life or style of life ever possible as a direct intention, or does one simply design environmental factors in such a way that the Holy Spirit is ultimately responsible, in relationship with the individual, for her or his formation? Finally, if catechesis is an effort made by ministers of God's Word, how is the term "minister" being used? Are not catechists then ministers? What does this do to the understanding of priesthood within the church as it has been assumed up to the very recent past?

Sensitivity to these problems places many parish personnel in a dilemma which has yet to be worked out in practice. It also leads to the presence of a third framework, observable in many places, where the two preceding frameworks are brought together in a not wholly integrated manner. This third framework is one where educators tend to accept the positive aspects of catechesis, and catechists the positive aspects of education, seeing themselves as catechist-teachers or educational ministers. The presupposition such a position appears to indicate is that there is actually no difference between pastoral ministry and religious education, and that they are somehow interchangeable. Yet, semantically, education and ministry are not synonomous terms. In the long run, this last seems to be least feasible, because of the absence of distinctions; the second appears somewhat narrow, and the first the most comprehensive. However, individual Coordinators must ultimately work out their own understandings in their own situations. Although my own prefer-

7. See Gabriel Moran, *The Present Revelation*, New York: Herder and Herder, 1972, p. 19.

ence is for the first framework, the entire question is raised here not so much as an apologia for this position; rather, it is intended as a catalyst for serious reflection upon a fundamental issue.

QUESTION 2. *What valuing criteria does the Coordinator use to assess the parish educational task?*

In a paper published some time ago, Dwayne Huebner of Teachers College, Columbia University, raised the question of the valuing processes one uses to view educational activity. Huebner suggested five processes: technical, scientific, political, aesthetic and ethical.[8] He noted that all are necessary in educational activity, but that the first three tend to be used to the exclusion of the last two. Hence, looking at education technically, one tends to work in terms of means, ends, objectives and machines; viewing it scientifically, one tends to set up hypotheses and then conduct educational activity a certain way in order to test them; viewing education politically, one tends to structure educational activity in view of what some outside agent or agency demands, or to avoid certain practices because of the political ramifications. In how many religious education programs, for example, are decisions made or *not* made because parents or pastor or bishop would never allow them, instead of on either religious or educational grounds?

As has been remarked, one must at times view education technically, scientifically and politically, if only to avoid naiveté or the repetition of outmoded practices. But it may be of some value to the DRE to consider reflecting on parish educational activity through two other modes, the aesthetic and the religious: on the one hand, because they enlarge one's educational perspective; on the other, because they are more consonant with an area of life dealing with wonder, mystery and awe.

One can immediately note a correspondence between religious education and the aesthetic when one considers the ob-

---

8. "Curricular Language and Classroom Meanings," in *Language and Meaning*, ed. James McDonald and Robert Leeper, Washington: 1966. In this section, I shall substitute religious for ethical as more central to the question being raised here.

vious assertion that art makes possible understandings not expressible in discourse. Susanne Langer writes: "The most salient characteristic of discourse is that its symbolization of concepts is held to one dominant projection. . . . Other expressive devices may find their way into the pattern of discourse, but they are contingent to the basic pattern, and their sense is very aptly said to be 'between the lines.' "[9] The realities with which education in religion deals are often by their nature at least partially unspeakable, ineffable, incapable of verbal articulation, and, therefore, between the lines. There is an inner, personal knowledge of being, of human destiny, and of the presence of God which goes beyond words and which cannot be talked about. The aesthetic provides a threefold function in this case. In the first, it allows for expression of what is not articulable through language. In the second, it can complete incomplete verbal articulation by offering another modality. In the third, it can provide a vehicle for conceptualization in a way that is open to many interpretations or none, much in the same larger than life modes as myth and ritual. It would seem that in carrying out their educational roles, Coordinators would be greatly assisted by the use of such criteria. Looked at in another way, they might also be able to relax in their work with the acceptance of the freeing realization that in the area of religion, not everything needs saying, not everything is sayable, and that speech is not the only, or even the most adequate, means of human expression. In addition, this would seem to be an invaluable insight to convey to other teachers with whom they work.

Concerned as it is with the things of the earth, the aesthetic is a continual reminder of the bodily nature of human existence, and of the fact that humanity is nourished by soil, water, sunlight and fire. Despite the fact that human beings are often tempted to escape from the rhythm of their bodily life, this is neither possible nor desirable. To be concerned with human beings, as DRE's are called to be, is to be concerned with them wholly, and this means with their bodily life and the human and

9. Susanne Langer, *Mind: An Essay on Human Feeling*, Baltimore: The Johns Hopkins Press, 1967, Volume I, p. 102.

universal rhythms that help to constitute it. Furthermore, a religion including creation and incarnation would seem necessarily to be involved with human relationship to the world, how people live in it, and how they encounter those who inhabit it with them. What is being suggested here is the power of aesthetic reflection to make this earthly rootedness visible and apparent so that persons may be assisted to come to grips with their world. Coordinators who find that their educational work appears to carry them beyond a classroom or a learning session would, again, be helped by an understanding that, viewed aesthetically, religious education will always lead to a consideration of the world in which the people they are working with live, and to communal attempts to come to grips with the material universe.

Another way in which aesthetic criteria would prove valuable is by offering categories drawn from the world of art. What, for example, is the *design* of the educational experience? Is it possible for a course of study to be seen as a set of disparate elements like paint, brushes, color and canvas, but, in this case, people, subject matter, ongoing reflection and interaction, which may in the course of time become a completed work, along the lines of an artistic process which terminates in a completed art form? Does one care for and carry out responsibility for space as an artist must always do? And is the form and shape of the educational activity of equal importance to the materials used to embody it?

Similarly, one in the field of religious education might also bring specifically religious criteria to bear on the quality of educational activity. How, for example, does one carry on the religious process of judgment which is so often part of education? Do marks grade, or degrade, the human person? Is religious education conducted in order to lead to conversion, and, if so, what is the conversion toward? Is there always an awareness in the interactions between teachers and learners of the transcendent quality of each other's lives and of the undreamed of possibilities in all human life? Is faith at the root of the activity? Is hope? Is love?

Perhaps even more fundamentally, one engaged in religious

education would do well to reflect on the themes of death and resurrection which underlie much of human learning. Is there a death to positions or attitudes that are no longer adequate in a religious interpretation of the universe, and a corresponding movement toward resurrection to the new life that understanding and intelligence can facilitate? Is there a reverence toward the pain involved when people are faced with dying toward what they have always believed were fundamental values and must be reborn, with all the trauma of birth, to new vision? And at the heart of the enterprise, is there an unshakable resolve to respect the circle of freedom at the core of each human being, refusing to intrude, to manipulate, or to coerce? DRE's who bring aesthetic and religious criteria to bear on their own educational activity and on that of the persons with whom they work are living embodiments of Whitehead's hope for all education, and can take comfort in the realization that the foundation of their work is reverence for all of the human beings to whom they are related.

QUESTION 3. *What is the Coordinator's vision of the future of religious education?*

In speaking of the role of the diocesan office in chapter five, the suggestion was made that some time be spent in dreaming for the future. The same task is incumbent on the Coordinator. It is of major importance for Coordinators in their everyday educational role to have in mind a vision beyond what is now possible, a vision that will act as a guide for them in the present. The two previous questions in this chapter have been intended to lead toward the raising of this most fundamental question. How *does* the Coordinator view the future of religious education?

The church-related religious education that has provided us with much of our context thus far is undoubtedly in an indeterminate state. To attempt a redefinition of the field, as suggested by the first draft of the National Catechetical Directory, while using much of the old terminology has the built-in difficulty of such terminology calling up old images. Such images presuppose that the underlying question for Christianity in conducting education is how adults are to present church-related materials to young people, or engage in church-related activities with them in the hope that the latter will become practicing church members. "We are hung up on classroom study in church education. Just visit an average church and ask someone to show you its educational program. . . . In most cases, you will be taken to Sunday morning classes where most likely an adult will be telling children and youth about Christian beliefs and customs."[10] Two related but distinct considerations emerge from this description. One is whether, if a person is attempting to arrive at a future vision, the same terminology as used in the past is any longer possible. The DRE must first ask, then, whether to change the nomenclature and revise the images. The second consideration runs deeper. It is the inquiry: What actually *is* the underlying question for Christianity in conducting educational programs? Is it the question presupposed by the prevailing images? Or is it a question on a totally different level?

Coordinators appear to be arriving at a vision where the question is indeed a different one from that which has up to now impelled church education. The great question for Christianity today is not the instruction of potential church members, but what the nature of the Christian church will be in the future. This question in turn is situated within the wider question of the relationship of Christianity to all other religions and non-religions which seek to move forward the human enterprise. The need that arises then is to find some universal point of view, some context from which to study religion in the changed historical circumstances where people find themselves. Such a context might be one that assumes it is no longer just a reworking of Christianity that is needed. Rather, it would be the concern: How is human experience, both religious and non-religious, related to Christianity in the framework of a world history where the church is no longer central? Any other context is quite possibly too intramural for these times. There appears to be a need,

---

10. John Westerhoff, *Values for Tomorrow's Children*, Philadelphia, Pilgrim Press, 1970, p. 40.

then, for a future religious education which is more universal, broader, and more catholic.

I would like to suggest that such a future vision of religious education would be characterized in the first place by the word human. If something is to be defined as human, in this case religious education, then it would need to have the same characteristics as the human. It would be fleshly and organic; it would be alive; it would be situated in time and space. At the same time, however, it would recognize, as aesthetic and religious criteria would impel it to do, that what constitutes the human is always in question, in the sense that it is yet to be, and always to be discovered. Ultimately, it would be an acknowledgment of the religious mystery of the Incarnation where the paradoxical and ineffable affirmation is that to be human is to be divine.

This religious education would also be related to the search for truth. Such truth, however, would be not so much the truth of fact where the opposite of a true statement is a false statement or even where some things are false and others are true. It would be rather the truth of art, where some things are adequate and others more adequate, and where the opposite of a profound statement may be, paradoxically, another profound statement. Its concern would not be arriving at right answers, but arriving at tentative solutions, or models, on the right kind of grounds.

This kind of religious education would also be without boundaries, limits, or pre-determined content. In the study of religion as a substantive cultural phenomenon, in the study of the religious as a characteristic quality of all experience, or in the study of one's own church's religious understanding, the evaluative criteria for testing its integrity as education might very well include aesthetic and religious reflectors such as those suggested above, as well as an inclusion of pre-verbal, supra-verbal and non-verbal expression, a non-dominative reverence toward the material environment of the world and the educational environment of the classroom, and a conscious but delicately balanced approach to the limitless thinking/feeling unity which constitutes the human person.

Coordinators and other parish personnel are aware that religious education as carried on in the present is not always this kind of enterprise. Instead, it is often directed toward the setting up of "religious experiences" and the discussion of religious questions with the goal almost always including some element of institutional self-preservation. What then might be the starting points for this kind of religious education? Two are suggested here: the centrality of human freedom and the adult character of religious education.

QUESTION 4. *How does the DRE view the issue of human freedom?*

If discussion of religious education were to begin from the fact of the centrality of human freedom, it would be working from the widest possible base. Educators and catechists would then be more inclined to approach their task using far fewer words than they do now, since most of their words are generally at the point of their own presuppositions rather than at the point of the learner's questions. The point is that no teacher, as remarked above, can *form* another's freedom; he or she is more likely to diminish it by working too hard to make it grow. The best that teachers can do is to attempt by an indirect kind of communication to help others discover what they are called to be. This presupposes, of course, the need for teachers with special qualities, and DRE's would do well to note, in their selection of teachers, whether such qualities are present.

The result of the presence of such teachers would be a change in the kind and amount of religious input included in courses in the parish. Teaching a fixed content of doctrine or scripture is not necessarily the way to true understanding, or to the response, creativity and involvement claimed as the objectives of genuine religious education. It can often lead, on the contrary, to the mutilation of understanding, or even to an antireligious attitude. This is especially true when the text is presented first instead of as the expression of an understanding that has been given time to mature through several levels of learning, and through several kinds of experience, such as community or liturgy.[11]

If freedom were the central concern, there would also be a more profound reverence for the power of the human person to arrive at her or his own conclusions. One of the fundamental conditions for such understanding would certainly be the creation of an environment where this activity could take place. The ideal would be if this attitude were present in all education, and although the religious education efforts of the parish could not effect that result single-handedly, it could certainly contribute significantly toward its accomplishment in the general field of education.

QUESTION 5. *How does the DRE view the adult character of religious education?*

It would seem that if a parish wishes to devise structures for learning that issue from a concern for freedom, there would have to be a shift of resources. Religious study, and the money and facilities available for conducting it, is still largely a child-centered operation. Primary attention is almost always given to the child's education in religion or to the way adults relate themselves to that education. This does not mean that Parish Coordinators should ignore the religious education of children, but it does raise the question of whether the present structure of child, teen-age and adult programs in parishes, with emphases on the first two, is the best way to help children toward an understanding of the religious quality of their lives. Many DRE's will observe that the education of children in their own parishes is inevitably too cognitive, too verbal and too little concerned with the child's actual experience, and their problem becomes the discovery of ways in which this might be changed. They are on to the insight that, quite simply, children have not lived long enough to rationally inquire into the nature of human life, the universe and God, in the style presumed by systematic theology

---

11. I am reminded here of T. S. Eliot's comment in "The Dry Salvages": "We had the experience but missed the meaning." See *Four Quartets*, New York: Harcourt, Brace and Company, 1943, p. 24.

and still evident in too many textbooks. Instead, children's religious attitudes and questions are diffused throughout their entire experience. The emphasis on home programs where one person learns together with a small group of eight or ten children is an acknowledgment of the realization that children need adults who will help them become aware of and accepting of their own feelings, and will guide them through their changing language patterns and ideas as they grow older. Such education for children is one explanation of what is meant by adult-directed or adult-oriented education: the child is being helped toward adulthood.

Adults are different from children since they are persons who have experienced something of the nature of faith, who ask questions concerning ultimate realities such as death and life, and who wish to understand their particular religious and/or Christian tradition on intelligent grounds. They are ready for religious study and for profound explanation of doctrine. That study, however, must be carried on with intellectual honesty, without indoctrination or proselytizing, and by teachers who are themselves co-learners. It therefore falls more and more into the province of the DRE to devise models, objectives and ideals for the adult who wishes serious education in the area of religion. Such models will certainly be different from past models that have tended to treat adults as if they were children.

Critical to the continuing education of adults is the presence of someone who is a facilitator of their learning. In chapter five it was noted that adults are quite capable of taking care of their own learning; nevertheless, someone who is present as a catalyst or resource person for this learning may be of great assistance. Persons who act as catalysts for, or facilitators of, adult learning need to be confident of their own processive, maturing, individuality, and to be characterized by discipline, openness, readiness to learn with the community, humility and enthusiasm. It is particularly helpful if they are excited about learning and about life, and eager to share this understanding of life and learning with others. But of paramount importance is that they be people who can help others be in touch with their own resources and with the resources in their environment.

Finding such persons and working with them in order to improve education in the parish is a major role for the DRE, and the discovery of such persons is a fundamental need if religious education in parishes is to move toward a different future. It is toward the articulation of those questions which will aid in the discovery of such persons that the next chapter is directed, as well as toward an understanding of the personal questions underlying teaching that we now turn.

**STRATEGY NO. 23: STATING YOUR PHILOSOPHY
OF RELIGIOUS EDUCATION**

You have been asked by the Religious Education Association to define religious education as you understand it, and to sketch what you see as its most important components. To do so, you are asked to answer each of the following questions in a statement of no more than 100 words.

1. What is your definition of religious education?

2. What is your future vision of religious education? What would you like religious education in your parish to look like ten years from today?

STRATEGY NO. 24: THE DRE'S BASIC FRAMEWORK

Out of what basic framework do you view the work of religious education for yourself: education; pastoral ministry; a combination of these two; other? Give at least three reasons why you feel the framework chosen is the most appropriate for you.

My basic framework:

My reasons:

1.

2.

3.

STRATEGY NO. 25: CHOOSING CRITERIA
TO ASSESS
RELIGIOUS EDUCATION

The following are five basic criteria. In each case, two questions viewing the activity from the particular point of view named are suggested. The Coordinator is asked to select three more, along the lines delineated in this chapter.

TECHNICAL:

1. What behavioral objectives do I wish students to achieve?
2. What materials will I need to help students achieve them?
3.
4.
5.

SCIENTIFIC:

1. What new methodology might I use with students to achieve a different kind of learning situation?
2. On what basis do I know this methodology might be of help?
3.
4.
5.

POLITICAL:

1. In what ways is my activity with my teachers determined by my immediate superiors?
2. In what ways, if any, do I seek to exercise power over my co-workers?
3.
4.
5.

AESTHETIC:

1. What is the design of the educational program in my parish?

2. What kind of allowance do I make for both physical and psychological space in this program?

3.

4.

5.

RELIGIOUS:

1. In what ways does my religious education program reflect my belief in the religious quality of people's lives?

2. What provision do I make for death when it occurs in the learning lives of the people I teach?

3.

4.

5.

8
Education:
The Personal Framework

We consider now a number of questions that DRE's might ask of themselves and prospective teachers in order to discover how they look at the teaching act. People ordinarily bring certain presuppositions toward any activity in which they are engaged. These color and affect the way the activity is carried on. Often, however, such presuppositions remain at a sub-conscious or non-conscious level. This is particularly true for teachers who, although they may spend years of involvement in educational practice, are often hard put to articulate the nature of what they do or give it specific definition. The suggestion is made here that the following questions can provide assistance in discovering the underlying assumptions and attitudes that determine precisely how teaching is carried on in the parish. All of the questions have been asked of DRE's by the author innumerable times, and in most cases they have proven revelatory and helpful to them in coming to an understanding of their personal view of teaching.

QUESTION 1. *What synonyms do you associate with the word "teaching" and what feelings do you associate with teaching?*

The question is one which DRE's are asked to answer "off the top of their heads" before they read further. Right now, what are the words that most clearly help you explain to yourself the activity of teaching? Secondly, what feelings do you associate with carrying on the activity? How do you feel when you are doing it?

These questions almost always call forth positive responses.

Thus, in speaking of synonyms, that is, in trying to find other words that describe what goes on while one is teaching, responses tend to include "guiding," "facilitating," "encouraging," "sharing," "helping," "understanding" and "discovering."

In addressing the feelings associated with teaching, the responses are similarly positive. Teachers will indicate feelings such as enjoyment, exhilaration, excitement, and, often, "discomfort." The last, however, is not necessarily felt as negative. Instead, when teachers are asked to say more about this feeling, they tend to focus on the familiar experience of uneasiness that often accompanies genuine learning, and the defensiveness that sometimes appears in a new situation where one is both attracted and repelled at the same time. This is significant of what is undoubtedly an educational truism: all genuine learning involves some discomfort, because it calls for a shift of vision, a leaving of an old position, and a readjustment of one's view of reality.

An interesting strategy to use in the asking of this question is to query oneself and/or one's teachers by turning the question around to be: "Now, what words or feelings do you think students would have given in response to this question?" Invariably, although there are many positive responses, one word tends to predominate whenever the question is put this way. It is the word "boring." The response is intriguing. Why do teachers assume that students are bored by teachers, which means wearied by dullness or tedious repetition? Why is it assumed that teaching, in the view of students, is dull and tiresome? If teachers are pressed, they do admit that the boredom they attribute to students is with particular age groups, especially learners who are between ten and eighteen. Generally, young children are not thought of as bored, nor are adult learners.

This response may be indicative of a number of important educational considerations. The first is that with young children, teachers tend to use a variety of methodologies, particularly bodily involvement and manipulation of materials. With adults, the learners are there because they want to be. Perhaps there is some truth to the educated guess of many in religious education that with the ten to eighteen group, one is better advised to address religious concerns in other ways than formal teaching situations, a guess borne out by the phenomenal success of youth retreats as the major church education effort with youth. At any rate, fundamental to the raising of this and the following question is the accompanying one that it is wise to ask before proceeding: "What does your answer mean in terms of your personal teaching activity?"

QUESTION 2. *Why did you start to teach?*

With prospective teachers who have never taught, the question might be phrased differently as "Why do you want to teach?" but the point of the question is to help teachers articulate the reasons why they began or wish to begin teaching. Many members of religious orders, for example, will respond that they did not begin to teach because they wished to be involved in education; their initial desire was to be a nun or a brother, and being a nun or brother meant that one became involved in the work of a particular congregation, which in the United States was often a teaching order. Such persons are generally quick to add, however, that once they became seriously involved in teaching as a profession, they found that it was a congenial and happy one, and one that they learned to love.

A number of other responses often surface. One is that the person has a genuine love of children and young people. Interestingly, although most DRE's note that they enjoy working with adults better than with children, the underlying notion that appears when these questions are asked is of an activity where one works with the young in a learning situation. This is significant in that it helps teachers to examine whether one relates differently, as a teacher, with children and with adults, if one sees himself or herself as a co-learner with one group but not with the other, and whether there is a bias and/or a prejudice toward children operative in the way their education is carried on, as distinguished from a freer atmosphere in adult learning situations.[1] Nevertheless, the response that indicates genuine love

---

1. For discussion of societal biases toward children and the entire question of children's rights, see Richard Farson, *op. cit.* See also John Holt, *Escape from Childhood*, New York: Dutton, 1974.

and concern for young people is an important one. It is not unknown that people who work with children sometimes do not really like or understand them, and no attitude is more easily communicated to the young than this one.

Another response that is significantly positive is that of someone who wants to teach or began teaching because of his or her own positive educational experiences. Often, teachers will cite the presence of a teacher in their own lives who made learning such a joy for them that they grew up wanting to do the same thing for others. Particularly impressive is the person who grew up having difficulty learning, who understands how hard it can sometimes be, and who does not want others to have the same experience.

With a new group of prospective teachers in a parish, most times the answers are manifold and wide-ranging. Often Coordinators will duplicate the responses for a beginning group of teachers to give them some understanding of why the others are there. A sample list might include such responses as:

"I heard an announcement from the pulpit and wanted to help the parish."

"I had free time on my hands and wanted to do something with it."

"I want to understand what is happening in my own child's religious education."

"The Coordinator came to my house and asked me to help."

"I had a friend who got me interested in the program."[2]

Generally, the responses change as people become involved in the actual teaching situation. However, it might be noted here that when one is starting, the support of others is invalu-

---

2. The response that has always intrigued me most was that of the woman who answered: "I wanted to do to other people's children what they had done to mine."

able. One student of mine, a Diocesan Director of the Latin American Apostolate, shared a fine suggestion when discussion of this question was going on. He noted that when he was in Mexico all new personnel were assigned to someone who had been in the parish program for several years. The new teacher was always contacted prior to the first meetings, and the invitation extended, "We are going to the teachers' meeting you are attending tonight, and would like to stop by for you at seven-thirty." Such concern is invaluable to the person who has not yet begun to teach, or is not yet sufficiently involved in the program to be on her or his own.

QUESTION 3. *Why do you remain in teaching?*
As soon as involvement begins in earnest, the responses and attitudes begin to change. If people remain in teaching, either as paid professionals or as volunteers, it is almost always because they like working with people, they are inspired and challenged by the activity, they are encouraged by seeing growth and change in other human beings, and they feel that they are doing something valuable with their lives. They may have questions as to whether they are using appropriate methodologies; they may encounter difficulties where students misunderstand the entire context of a discussion ("She told me it was perfectly all right to miss Sunday Mass"), they may be periodically discouraged because of apparent lack of cooperation or non-involvement by those in administrative roles. Nevertheless, particularly with persons who volunteer to teach in the religious education program, DRE's find a commitment and dedication that is remarkable. Where this involvement occurs, there appear to be several accompanying reasons. One is that the new teachers are not simply told to jump into the teaching water with the injunction: "Swim!" Instead, they receive constant, regular, well-planned and careful assistance from the DRE or his or her co-workers in preparation of classes. They experience a sense of community with the other teachers that is often lacking in the suburban structure of detached homes, or in big-city anonymity. They find that the religious content they are engaged with is enlarging their own learning lives in ways they had not antici-

pated. Finally, they often discover in the person of the Parish Coordinator a priestly, counseling sister or brother who represents to them an important connection with the church which has not always been present in their experience.

QUESTION 4. *From whose side of the desk do you prepare your teaching?*
This question may appear to be a throwaway question which needs little explanation, but it is not. It was suggested to me by a woman who had worked on a team of DRE's for eight years and then had decided to return to college to complete her bachelor's degree. She noted that when she returned to the other side of the desk, after having been a director of learning for so long, she was appalled by the number of professors whose intent was obviously to cover material with no attempt to understand who the learners were, what their backgrounds were, or what questions, if any, they were bringing to the situation. What the question points to, of course, is the danger always lurking in a teaching situation: that of seeing it as a one-way street. But the question also invites the reflection that in one's preparation there must always be a carefully planned use of language and examples that touch the learners' lives, and an understanding that if one is observing someone in a teaching situation (or listening to or viewing a tape of oneself), key clues that indicate whether teaching is going on are whether there is support and mutuality, and whether, most critically, teacher and students are using language either in the same way, or in a way where one understands the meanings being communicated by the language of the other.

It has already been remarked that church people are prone to use "incensy" language. This is true not only of sermons, but of teaching situations where the content is religious. A seminarian engaged in field work, teaching a class of fifteen-year olds about the meaning of Easter, may be tremendously excited about the celebration of the event as it is planned at the seminary, but if he or she speaks of "the Great Triduum that precedes the re-enactment of the Paschal Event" as I have heard done in one situation, he or she has lost the group and obfuscation has set in. Awareness of what it is like on the other side of the desk can obviate such occurrences. It can also cause the teacher to ask whether there should indeed *be* a piece of furniture between learners, or whether most genuine learning will go on in a physical environment that is circular instead of set in a pattern of straight lines where all persons but one face the same direction.

QUESTION 5. *Cite three positive educational experiences you had before you were fifteen.*

Returning to the principle of positive motivation, this question invites DRE's and teachers to reflect on their own learning when they were young. Stress on the word *positive* is directed to those learning situations remembered as fruitful ones, although it is to be remembered that there are many we will tend to forget. Stress on the word *educational* is intended to convey the understanding that the experience need not be connected with school (though school is not to be automatically excluded). Most people will remember experiences other than in school in at least one or two of their examples, and such recollection is one of the best ways to disabuse people of the notion that education and schooling are equivalent, as well as one of the best devices to reflect on the differences between formal and informal education.

Almost always (DRE's are invited to confirm the following observation by their own asking of the question), responses will fall into one of three categories. The first set of responses are ones that incorporate bodily involvement, which often will have a connection with art. People will remember learning to play a musical instrument, singing in a chorus, playing Barbara Frietchie in a play about the American Revolution, learning to swim, discovering the ability in themselves to tell time, nature study hikes, field trips to Kennedy Airport or the Grand Canyon. The point the educator can make in reflecting on these responses with teachers is that young people learn best when there is involvement of their whole persons. One could approach this truth by sharing Piaget's insights about the stages of cognitive development, but to begin by dealing with one's own educational history is almost always a better introduction to Piaget, and a buttress to study of his monumental contribution.[3] The connection these experiences so often have with painting, acting, singing or playing an instrument will confirm those teachers who suspect they are right in including student participation whenever possible, but still feel pangs of guilt when they do not cover all the material assigned. It can also cause them to consider whether, even if they *are* covering material, particularly cognitive material, any learning is actually going on if unrelated to actual student involvement and experience.

A second set of responses tends to be in the recollection of some teacher or significant adult, such as a parent, who would not accept inferior work from the person when they were young, but who pushed them back, instead, to their own resources, and toward the discovery of possibilities in themselves that they had not previously acknowledged or even knew were there. What the teacher did in the first place was to actually *see* the young person, to recognize her or his uniqueness, and to press her or him to work out the situation by using the resources found in her or his own person. Dr. Mary Tully, formerly of the faculty of Union Theological Seminary in New York, once supplied a marvelous example of this kind of teacher. She noted that a child might come to its father and say, "My bicycle is broken," and that the father could respond in one of two ways. The first would be to say, "I'll fix it." The second, however, would be a sign that the father was a teacher. It would be the response, "What do *you* think we can do to fix it?" "How shall we go about it?" When young people meet the second kind of adult, they tend to have positive educational experiences that are remembered throughout their lives.

A third set of responses is the remembrance of incidents where learning took place because the young persons themselves took on the role of teacher. The educational truism that one learns best when one has to teach something oneself is surpris-

---

3. For a fine introduction for one unfamiliar with Piaget, see Molly Brearley and Elizabeth Hitchfield, *A Guide to Reading Piaget*, New York: Schocken Books, 1966.

ingly inoperative when adults conduct learning sessions with young people. It would seem that far more could be done in setting up situations where children teach other children, older children assist younger children with difficulties and problems, and multi-age groupings of children are used as a fertile source for education. David and Margaret Steward have written, "We hypothesize that when first-born children serve as teachers to their younger siblings, they are given an opportunity to repeat the tasks they have to teach to the point where they really master them."[4] The description of Open Corridor Learning in New York City documents a similar experience where students notice others having difficulty and assist them as a matter of course.[5] Any DRE who has had extensive involvement in Open Classroom situations can confirm this experience.

What is to be hoped, whatever the responses to this question (and it is suggested that they be dittoed or written on a blackboard as they are shared so that people may see the threefold pattern of responses emerging), is that the answers will confirm for both teachers and Coordinators much about learning that they already know intuitively, and be a support for them in their educational activity with young people.

QUESTION 6. *Cite three positive educational experiences you have had as an adult.*

This question has similar phraseology to the one preceding, but the emphasis here is on the changes in what is considered positively educational as one grows older. There is now far more ability to reflect rationally, not only because one's powers of thought and abstraction have developed, but also because one's experience as an adult is so much more vast than a child's. Many of the teachers with whom DRE's work will not have attended college; others will have had courses at the undergrad-

4. See "Early Learning in the Family: A Report of Research in Progress," in *Character Potential*, Schenectady: Union College Character Research Project, Volume 6, No. 4, February 1974, p. 175.

5. See Lillian Weber, "Education for ALL the Children," in *Notes from Workshop Center for Open Education*, New York: 1974, pp. 2-20.

uate or graduate level that have significantly changed their lives. Thus, examples will vary depending on background.

Despite a wide range of background, however, the nature of what is considered a positive educational experience in adult life tends to be remarkably similar. The first is contact with a particular person who in some way brought one to an experience of integration. The integration itself may be of ideas, or, at a deeper level, of one's entire life. On the one hand, it may be articulated as contact with a teacher who spoke in such a way that the learner could say, "Ah! So that's what was happening," or "Now I understand how the whole thing fits." The other is usually a more intimate experience such as falling in love or marrying, where intimacy with another person called forth human qualities that had until then been dormant and caused the person to have a more complete sense of him- or herself.

Where the adult educational experiences were in a formal setting such as college, the emphasis still appears to be on personal qualities in the teacher, and the qualities themselves tend to be reducible to enthusiasm, insight and thorough preparation. Over and over, adults will recall someone who, though a teacher in an area not initially of concern to the learner, communicated such excitement about the field that it "caught" and the learner was initiated into a new dimension of existence. Or they will mention the quality of insight, where material that was thought to be familiar was illuminated in a new and surprising way by someone who had the artistic gift of putting elements together to form a new whole. Finally, adults are always cognizant of the teacher who is thoroughly prepared and who is never found guilty of the subtle insult conveyed in taking people's time and money without adequate and responsible return.

QUESTION 7. *How do you distinguish between content and method?*

Like body and soul or thought and feeling, education is plagued by a dichotomy that tends to separate two elements that are logically distinct, yet inseparable in practice: content and method. As soon as one changes the word method to process, there is a certain relaxation, since method tends to convey the almost universally negative experience of student teachers in taking "methods" courses. Furthermore, recent educational thinking has tended to emphasize the realization that process *is* in some way content, and Marshall McLuhan's dictum that the medium is the message has become so much a part of cultural lore that it is accepted without question.

Nevertheless, beginning teachers need to be assisted to see that content is not the most important part of their educational task, although neither is method or process. The paradoxical understanding is that they form a unity and cannot exist without one another. It is the acceptance of this ambiguity that the DRE must try to instill in beginning teachers. All educating persons need to be disabused of the notion that content is something that students come to "get" and that it does not much matter how it is gotten. Of this problem Neil Postman and Charles Weingartner have written:

> To our knowledge, all schools of education and teacher-training institutions in the United States are organized around the idea that content and method are separate. . . . Perhaps the most important message thus communicated to teachers in training is that this separation is real, useful, and urgent, and that it ought to be maintained. . . . A secondary message is that, while the "content" and "method" are separate, they are not equal. Everyone knows that the "real" courses are the content courses.[6]

In parish religious education, particularly, this dichotomy must be overcome. Education by a community for a community will always depend on the quality of that community's life and its style of communication far more than on its verbalization of doctrine. To overcome the content-method dichotomy, then, is a primary concern for DRE's and their teaching staff.

---

6. In *Teaching as a Subversive Activity*, New York: Dell Publishing Co., 1969, p. 18.

QUESTION 8. *How do you distinguish between method, style, skill and control?*

Once the content-method question has been addressed, Parish Coordinators and teachers can look together at another set of distinctions which need to be made in the examination of the teaching act. In an article entitled "On the Anatomy of Teaching," B. Othanel Smith asks his readers to reflect on the distinctions existing between these four words,[7] all of which recur constantly in discussion and practice of teaching.

It is to be noted that there are an infinite variety of methods or processes available to every teacher. For example, in *Adult Education Procedures*, Bergevin, Morris and Smith list fourteen educational techniques including colloquy, committee, demonstration, field trip, forum and panel, as well as six sub-techniques such as audience reaction teams, buzz sessions, idea inventories and screening panels.[8] The unreflective attitude toward method, however, tends to keep teachers from realizing the unlimited kinds of procedures available to them as teaching vehicles. In fact, most teachers tend either to teach as they were taught, or to rely almost exclusively on lecture, a method, one might remark, that is exceedingly difficult to master, the gift of very few, and often found in a diluted form which might be better labeled "article reading." A lecture, when it is a genuinely artistic teaching form, is not a discourse read *to* a group, but, rather, organized reflection that proceeds with almost mathematical precision from introduction to body to conclusion. At its best, it resembles the movements of a symphony, where unifying themes bind the whole together, and where changes in tempo, color, mood and tone quality bring one finally to a sense of completedness.

---

7. In *The Journal of Teacher Education*, Vol. VII, No. 4, December 1956.

8. See Paul Bergevin, Dwight Morris and Robert Smith, *Adult Education Procedures*, New York: Seabury, 1963. For far more extensive coverage of the nature and elements of teaching, see Bruce Joyce and Marsha Weil, *Models of Teaching*, Englewood Cliffs: Prentice-Hall, 1972 and Thomas Green, *The Activities of Teaching*, New York: McGraw-Hill, 1971.

What the DRE can assist teachers to do is to discover what teaching method (or what set of methods) is best for them, and then assist them in developing their own style, with style defined as "the characteristic demeanor in which the teaching acts are performed . . . personal and somewhat unique for each individual."[9] One's teaching style is much like one's handwriting, and beginning teachers need to be encouraged to play with several styles, trying them on for fit to find out which ones suit them best. Like handwriting, it will be understood that at first there will be some awkwardness, until a genuine and recognizable style is developed. The Coordinator might think of himself or herself here as analogous to a swimming instructor; at the beginning, before one learns to swim, it is very comforting to have a hand under one's stomach in order to keep from sinking. The objective, however, is to learn to swim on one's own. Eventually, the instructor removes the hand. DRE's need to convey the assurance that they will be around to keep their novice teachers from drowning in the frightening waters of first teaching experience, but as soon as the teachers begin to float, and then to move into deeper water, they are into the procedure of developing their own teaching style.

With practice comes skill, that is, the ability coming from knowledge *and* practice to perform with excellence, competence and dexterity. All teachers need to be aware that skill does not come automatically, but that repeated activity, willingness to take risks, reflection on the activity with a master teacher or group of teachers, and periodic conferences with students concerning their perceptions will almost certainly promote it. Probably it is true that some teachers will not be able to perform with skill, but they may be able to perform adequately. Furthermore, skill is not always of primary importance, especially when the students are young, fragile and impressionable. It may be of far more value to them to know that there is someone present who cares about them, and who realizes how important they are as individuals.

Control is mentioned here because, so often, beginning

---

9. B. Othanel Smith, *loc. cit.*, p. 340.

teachers see it as part of the teaching act itself, rather than as an accompaniment to the situation. In its limited sense, control indicates dominance, regulation, or command, and many beginning teachers will be under the impression that this is one of their major objectives. It may be far more important for them, however, to control their own predetermined notions of how education takes place, and to create an unfrozen atmosphere where students are free to develop at their own pace and discover their own gifts under guidance. Control becomes less of a consideration the older the educatee; the two places it is of most importance are in helping the very young to deal with impulses, fears or feelings that may frighten them because they do not know how to handle them, and with *situations*, rather than people, which are damaging or unproductive.

QUESTION 9. *What does it mean to teach?*

All of the foregoing questions have been intended to bring DRE's and their teachers to the point where they can actually ask this question. Having reflected on their own educational experience, and having examined some of the major components of the teaching act, the question may now be tentatively raised. What is it that one does when she or he engages in the act of teaching?

Even a cursory examination of writing in the area of teaching will indicate that there is no one definition acceptable to everyone. There are, at one end of the spectrum, persons like Carl Rogers who state, "My experience has been that I cannot teach another person how to learn,"[10] and others who go further in their opinion that nobody can teach anybody anything.[11] On the other hand, one's experience generally indicates that there have been teachers in one's life who have done *something* that in some way has engendered learning. Perhaps, therefore, only a very general definition can be helpful. A teacher, perhaps, is an agent or a community which structures the environment in such

10. See *Freedom To Learn*, Columbus: Charles E. Merrill, 1969, p. 152.

11. W. R. Wees. *Nobody Can Teach Anyone Anything*, Garden City: Doubleday, 1971.

a way that persons can get in touch with their own resources and the resources around them (one of which may be the teacher) toward the future.

The concern with structuring the environment appears to be a critical element. Another way of saying this is that a teacher is one who designs curriculum. What must be mentioned as a caution here, however, is the myopic view of curriculum that still pervades much educational understanding. In most parishes where the term curriculum is used, it is generally in a sentence such as, "If we could only find the right curriculum," meaning in practice, "Shall we use Benziger, Shalom, Sadlier, Paulist or Hi-Time?" This notion of curriculum focuses on its least important aspect, and the one that is last in order of importance. For curriculum has at least a fivefold meaning: (1) the physical environment itself, based on the belief that *where* people learn determines to a great extent what and how they learn; (2) the interaction curriculum, that is, all the relationships impinging on the learning situation such as: administration-teacher, teacher-administration, teacher-teacher, student-teacher, teacher-student, teacher-students, teachers-students, student-student, and students-students; (3) the private curriculum, that is, the *inside* of both teacher and student, the presuppositions, convictions, moods, prejudices and prior experience they bring to the situation; (4) the community curriculum, that is, the kind of community from which the persons come, the community existing in the learning situation (if any does in fact exist), as well as the wider local, state, national and world community, and (5) the academic resources or knowledge resources that assist in the entire process, for example, the texts, films, materials and machines. It is this much, at least, which is incorporated in the idea of curriculum.

Helping persons to get in touch with their own resources is another component of the teaching activity. It is very much related to the design of the learning environment and to the aesthetic criteria mentioned in chapter seven. If a carefully designed learning environment is set up, it places the student in the stance of an artist. In such a situation, there is a lack of pressure to work or to learn on someone else's terms. Students are enabled to do what they need to do and are not pressured to find a particular meaning. This is a difficult procedure, for even when newer modes of education are devised, there is always the danger that the learner will not be asked to search for his or her own truth, but instead to handle data already arrived at and return it unchanged and intact to the instructor. When the environment does help in discovering one's own resources and meaning, as is the case when the environment is aesthetically conceived, then it is possible for religious questions to be consciously, but still individually, addressed, through learners tapping their own resources and those around them.

In speaking of this kind of learning, Mary Tully once noted of herself as a teacher of art:

> I'm assuming that my job is to help students, through art, to make some sense of the content they're already getting, or have had. My experience has been that most of these young people have had so much input that has not been digested that it's really a form of indigestion. And they need an area—and I think art is marvelous for this—where they can in secret, without somebody bothering them, integrate some of this material.[12]

Although teachers of religion provide religious content, rather than teach art, they need always to have methodological correctives such as those just mentioned if their teaching is to bear fruit.

The element of directing the activity of teaching toward the future leads finally to Question 10, which is the place to conclude this set of personal questions related to teaching.

QUESTION 10: *What is education?*

Last in order here, the question is *the* primary one. If religious education is central to the role of the Parish Coordinator, then it is of major importance to bring all of his or her

---

12. In an interview with me on December 9, 1970.

powers of reflection to bear on this question. Whether one thinks of oneself as an educator, or as a pastoral minister in an educational role, the question cannot be bypassed, for it is critically important to the life not only of the parish, but of the entire church.

I should like to submit that in the long history of education, the definition of education most fruitful for the church in the United States is the one articulated by the foremost philosopher of this country, who, it is to be remembered, began his career as a Sunday School teacher. In *Democracy and Education*, John Dewey spoke of education in a way that, because of its breadth, is applicable to almost every learning situation one might encounter. Education, he wrote, is "that reconstruction or reorganization of experience, which adds to the meaning of experience, and which increases ability to direct the course of subsequent experience."[13]

One must of course be aware that when Dewey is speaking of experience, he is not speaking of the limited life experience of one person, or of those activities teachers design and then refer to as "experiences." "Experience is the result, the sign, and the reward of that interaction of organism and environment which, when it is carried to the full, is a transformation of interaction into participation and communication."[14] Ultimately, for Dewey, all human experience is social.[15] Thus, when education is looked upon as the reconstruction of experience, it is that of the entire human community, and the giving of meaning to experience is a communal task that learners must engage in together, out of the fabric of their own lives, out of the context of all those lives which have preceded them, and in a stream of continuity toward the future as well. When Parish Coordinators and the teachers who are their closest associates find meaning in the turbulent experience of their world, dipping back for suste-

---

13. New York: Macmillan, 1916, p. 76.
14. John Dewey, *Art as Experience*, New York: G. P. Putnam's Capricorn Book, 1934, p. 22.
15. John Dewey, *Experience and Education*, New York: Macmillan, 1938, p. 38.

nance into the rich religious well of meaning that has grown in their Judaeo-Christian tradition for thousands of years, there is every chance that together they will be able to direct the course of subsequent experience. Hopefully, they will come together to an understanding and a celebration of the nobility of this enterprise.

STRATEGY NO. 26: QUESTIONS FOR TEACHERS

1. What synonyms come to your mind in defining the word "teaching"?

2. What feelings do you associate with "teachers" and "teaching"?

3. Why did you start to teach?

4. Why do you remain in teaching?

5. From whose side of the desk do you prepare your teaching?

6. Do you think there should be a desk at which a teacher sits?

7. Cite three positive educational experiences you had before you were fifteen.

1.

2.

3.

8. Cite three positive educational experiences you have had as an adult.

1.

2.

3.

9. How do you define teaching?

10. How do you define education?

STRATEGY NO. 27: MAKING DISTINCTIONS
IN TEACHING

1. How do you distinguish—or do you distinguish—between content and method?

2. How do you distinguish—or do you distinguish—between method, skill, style and control?

3. How do you distinguish—or do you distinguish—between teaching, instructing, indoctrinating, propagandizing and lying? At what point does teaching end on this continuum?

4. How do you distinguish—or do you distinguish—between teaching, preaching, and catechizing?

5. How do you distinguish—or do you distinguish—between facilitating, guiding, evoking, listening, discovering and teaching?

STRATEGY NO. 28: REFLECTORS FOR TEACHERS AND FOR DRE'S

In observing teachers and sharing observations with them, or in jointly observing teaching via video tape, the following questions might be raised as important to the entire teaching act:

1. How would you describe the teacher's use of gestures and of other vehicles besides language generally?

2. Is there an appeal to personal experience on the part of either teacher or student?

3. Does the teacher's face reveal any non-verbal clues? What about students' facial expressions?

4. Are you able to pick up the mood of the teacher and students? How would you describe it? What about the mood of the situation itself?

5. What is the physical situation of teacher and students? How are they seated—or standing?

6. Student interactions among themselves; with teacher: What are they? What are they like?

7. Are there any group norms observable? Are there obvious leaders in the student group toward whom others look?

8. What kind of institutional norms are observable? Is the teacher intent on preserving institutional over personal values?

9. Do teacher and students use language the same way?

10. What kind of questioning is going on? Teacher to student? Student to teacher? Student to student? Just for information? Provocative, creative, e.g., "Suppose . . ." or "What if . . ."

11. What can you identify with reference to the tone of the situation? Tone of voices of teacher, students; tone of the entire discussion; tone of what is *not* said?

12. Are there any appeals to authority in the situation? If so, what kind?

13. Is the intention of the teacher clear from observation of the situation?

14. What of the number of persons in the learning situation? Are there too few? Are there too many? Should they be grouped differently? Should there be more than one teacher?

15. What do you notice about interactions outside the actual learning situation as structured? What, if anything, is going on during the break?

STRATEGY NO. 29: LESSON PLANNING

The DRE is invited to ask all of her or his teachers to share a lesson plan that designs curriculum, with the following questions filled in either before or after a learning session:

1. What is your plan for the design of the physical environment where the learning session is to take place? Can you visualize it beforehand? Do you know where all pieces of furniture and equipment will be placed? Do you have all the equipment necessary? Is there a rug?

2. Are there any notable or observable relationships holding you back, or encouraging you forward? Are there any notable or observable relationships impinging on learners?

3. Are you aware of your own presuppositions about the lesson and procedures you are about to (or have just) undertake(n)? Are you aware of the presuppositions and experiences the group is bringing, both individually, and as a group?

4. Is the group itself a group, or a community? How much are the persons in the learning session, including yourself, involved with one another; with the wider community?

5. What academic materials or knowledge resources have you chosen for the learning session? On what basis, and for what reasons have you chosen them? Have those you will be working with participated in any way in the choice of these resources?

9
Education: Alternative Frameworks

In crossing the country, one notices that the structure of the religious education programs conducted in parishes is quite similar. As remarked at the beginning of chapter two, walking in beaten paths is always easier than introducing a new order of conceptions. Nevertheless, if Coordinators are to function as educational change agents and raise the consciousness of parishioners to new issues, and new ways of doing things, it becomes necessary for them to introduce educational frameworks alternative to those now in existence. Of course there are parishes where alternatives are already in operation, but the vast majority of parish educational programs still run on the assumption that there is to be a structured program for children of elementary age, another for teens, and a third, which is far less clearly defined, for adults, who most times are parents of people eighteen and under. In many cases, such programs are directed to preparation for the first reception of Penance and the Eucharist or to the reception of Baptism and Confirmation, all of which, again, tend to keep the education child-centered.

This chapter is directed toward the suggestion that alternative frameworks exist which could help a new order of conceptions to come about. Some are dreams, some are already in operation, but all are immediately possible, with only the slightest shift in resources necessary in some cases, and no shift in others. The Coordinator is invited to reflect along with other parish personnel about whether the following are in operation already in her or his parish. If they or some forms of them are not, the question might then be raised, "If not, why not?" Finally, if the alternative framework makes sense, the Coordinator is invited to bring it to the attention of her or his pastor, parish council, and parishioners, and see what develops.

QUESTION 1. *What kind of programs exist for senior citizens and young children?*

There is growing evidence in parishes throughout the country that Coordinators realize the evidence of psychology and anthropology: the most religious times of one's life are one's earliest years, when religiousness, wonder and a sense of the sacred are diffused throughout dawning experience in a kind of primitive way; and one's mature and even golden years, when life becomes integrated, generativity or concern for succeeding generations becomes paramount, and one has achieved an attitude of acceptance and serenity toward the mystery of death.

Programs currently in existence *do* acknowledge the importance of both these stages of life. Preschoolers, at best, are introduced to the sense training, the artistic initiation and the lesson of silence of Montessori, to take one example.[1] Consider, for a moment, the religious quality of an experience Montessori describes as occurring after a silence game.

The children, after they had made the effort necessary to maintain silence, enjoyed the sensation, took pleasure in the *silence* itself. They were like ships safe in a tranquil harbour, happy in having experienced something new, and to have won a victory over themselves. . . . It was then that I learned that the soul of a child has its own reward, and its peculiar spiritual pleasures. After such exercises it seemed to me that the children came close to me, certainly they became more obedient, more gentle and sweet. We had, indeed, been isolated from the world, and had passed several minutes during which the communion between us was very close, I wishing for them and calling to them, and they receiving in perfect silence the voice which was direct-

---

1. Another example is the Paulist program, *Awakenings*.

ed personally toward each one of them, crowning each in turn with happiness.[2]

Parishes are also becoming involved in attempts to conduct programs for senior citizens. The awareness has dawned that the nighttime is the poorest time for programs for older people, and so they have recently tended to be scheduled for morning or early afternoon, either in parish buildings, or in the homes of the participants. As mentioned earlier, scripture is a topic of obvious concern, but so too is morality and the changing nature of the church. There is also a nurturant side effect of such programs; senior citizens are finally being given a detailed and explicit background in why things have changed as they have, and it thus becomes a fine opportunity for letting off steam that has accumulated since Vatican II.

What is not always offered, however, and what is suggested either as an alternative or an accompanying framework to the above is a plan where the young and the old are brought together. The suggestion is made partly on the basis of observing Foster Grandparent programs funded by the federal government in Broome County, New York, but, even more, as a pick-up on a suggestion made by Dr. Elisabeth Kubler-Ross, whose work with dying patients has brought her into close contact with the very young and with the old. Commenting in a television interview[3] on her own dreams for the future before she dies, Dr. Ross admitted that her own stage of bargaining will take the form of one request. It will be that every community establishes homes that are both day-care centers and residences or centers for older people at the same time. She points out that young and old need each other, although in our society the two tend to be isolated. Educationally, the older persons could love, learn with and listen to the young, even for as brief a period as fifteen minutes daily, while the young could be similarly engaged with the older persons. Dioceses and parishes throughout the country

---

2. Maria Montessori, *The Montessori Method*, New York: Schocken Books, 1964 (first published 1912), pp. 211-212.
3. NBC rebroadcast, August 10, 1975.

have certainly invested enough in the six to eighteen year olds of the church; it is a matter of justice that attention be given to those under six and those over sixty. What makes the giving of this attention fairly easy is that there are more and more abandoned church buildings which could be used precisely for this purpose, as schools and convents are closed or no longer used for their original purposes. In addition, the suggestion represents a view of informal education different from the school model so determinative of our understanding of education. This alternative model presumes that meaning can be given to experience and the future course of experience directed by the simple interaction of two groups of people who understand each other very well. One group has enormous resources of experience to be reconstructed and reorganized; the other is constantly at the edge of brand new experience. Such an alternative educational program would be an enormous sign of hope for the entire church, and certainly for the individual parish.

QUESTION 2. *What is the approach to sacramental programs in the parish's religious education?*

As noted above, parish sacramental programs are almost always child-centered. Although they are programs calling for participation by parents and their children, where parents must attend at least one session directed toward their own understanding, the aim is still toward the child's readiness, and the adult is brought in so that she or he may become aware of the changing theology of individual sacraments, reflect on her or his own sacramental life, and perhaps come to a new and more adult involvement in the church's sacramental system, but still in relationship with the child. One sign of this underlying belief is that invitations to attend sacramental preparation programs are generally not total parish invitations, but directed solely to parents.

Although such programs attempt to involve adults, they rarely start with the adult. The alternative sacramental framework suggested here is precisely that: one that takes its point of departure from the premise that sacramental understanding must begin with the adult, and then and only then work backward to the child as someone who is capable of very little cognitive reflection concerning such mystery, though at the same time experientially capable of tremendous, though unreflected, bodily involvement.

In reflecting on the nature of sacraments, the starting point would not be the seven sacraments, the reason being, of course, that the church has always insisted that all of life is sacramental, that every person and every thing can be a vehicle for the divine, and that those high points symbolized at birth, communion, human forgiveness, marriage and death are significant reminders of the sacramental possibility of all human existence. How much richer our understanding of sacraments might be if one began with the premise that everything was sacramental, rather than the narrow vision that only some parts of life are vessels for the holy!

This kind of understanding, as noted, is not wholly available to the child. She or he has not lived long enough to have a sense of the beauty of bodiliness that people who are artists or builders, who have borne a child, or who have celebrated their love through sexual intercourse know in the deepest centers of their being. Neither have children come to developed concepts of birth and death, which underlie so much of the church's sacramental life: Baptism as new life; Penance as forgiveness and reconciliation, the Eucharist as the life-affirming "heralding of the death of the Lord until he comes," the Anointing as a reminder of the communion between one's body and spirit in both the smaller deaths and births within life.

On the other hand, all in the church, adults and children, need assistance in dealing with two of the major problems holding back a richer interpretation of sacrament. One is the tendency to see sacraments as static realities, as reflected in such terminology as "outward sign." A sign is something one passes, a station or stopping point. In distinction, sacraments are of the quality of life itself; sacramental life is ongoing and continuous or it is not going on at all. One's baptism, for example, is not an event that was "way back there"; one was baptized into life, and is continually baptized throughout life; one is finally baptized into death. One is in process as a forgiving and forgiven person, but this too goes on continually, and certainly not just when one "goes to confession." (How often *do* people go to confession today, even with the new rite?) As a human being, one is called especially to communion with one's sisters and brothers, and so with God; it is this communion going on all the time that Holy Communion symbolizes: we, being many, are one bread. Theoretically, anyone who has studied religion or theology has little problem understanding such ideas. However, as long as the practice of sacramental preparation contines as it does in parishes, there will be little shift in actual understanding and types of initiating education.

What is suggested, therefore, is a total parish effort that begins with adult-centered emphasis on the sacraments. This might be done through the weekly liturgical celebration, through programs in homes, through ceremonies of adult renewal of baptismal promises other than at Easter, of anointing of the sick on Sunday afternoon at six-week intervals (a practice that has grown enormously over the past year and is reaching parishioners who had little involvement with the parish previously), through information-processing seminars directed toward opening up intelligent attitudes toward sacramentality, and by leaving the preparation of children for entrance into the sacramental life of the church completely in the hands of parents, who would hopefully be more able to do this, given such a parish sacramental program.

This would of course cause many DRE's and Parish Coordinators to wonder about their responsibility toward young people whose parents are not involved in church life, and to ask whether they ought to take on the education and initiation of such young people themselves. This decision is, of course, left to their own intelligence and judgment to make; there would seem, on the one hand, no reason why such could not be done; on the other, there is some question of how effective it would be if there were no reinforcement at home. I suspect most DRE's would opt for the former and trust as hard as they could in the Holy Spirit.

Most of all, however, there would undoubtedly be some need to move toward a de-clericalization of the sacraments as they are understood today in the church. One way of moving the notion from seven to everything as sacramental is to do so in tandem with the move toward the priesthood of all the people of God, so evident in scripture, and so continually referred to today. If the word "priest" meant a man or a woman, married or single, it would be difficult to have a separate hierarchical caste made up of those engaged in priesthood. If ordination were for a term, rather than a lifetime, persons in a community who obviously possessed a priestly charism could have that charism acknowledged for as long as both the person and the community mutually wished. More important for the purposes being raised here, there would not be a need to call in an outside agent when a community was celebrating a significant event in its own life. When one witnesses a woman who is a so-called "extraordinary" minister giving the Eucharist to her parents, even within the structure of the Mass as it exists today, or when one witnesses the father and mother of a newborn infant baptizing it themselves, some sense of the beauty and universality of sacramental power can be understood. One sees this sacramentality as symbolic of all the sacramentality such persons share together in their daily lives. Parish practice could do much to further this understanding, and those who are now ordained might well be the ones who could further it most, in cooperation with the Parish Coordinator.

What is of particular importance in discussion of this proposal is that it be understood as directed to the enrichment and fullness of both priestliness and sacramental life, and not to its dilution. Communities are always in need of those who will fulfill a priestly role, and human beings must always celebrate through bodily involvement where the spiritual is "matter and more," because they are bodily creatures. It would be a serious misrepresentation of what is being discussed here to read it as a call for an end to priesthood or the sacramental life of the church. It is, rather, a question of the more appropriate forms that priesthood and sacramentality might take in our culture.

QUESTION 3. *Does the parish articulate its educational program on a yearly basis?*

The legislative program of the Executive branch of the United States government is articulated yearly in the State of the Union address. Many states have an opening of the state legislature where the governor gives a State of the State address. Do parishes provide for their parishioners a description of their plans for the parish educationally, in a yearly State of the Parish address?

A State of the Parish program has a beginning, a middle and an end. The beginning involves the calling together of representatives of all communities within the parish, and a planning together of goals and objectives directed toward the bettering of the religious quality of the lives of its people. (Naturally, the parish program will include more than formal education, and the informal educational aspect of a State of the Parish program is a considerable one.) Such goals might be immeasurably diverse: the setting up of a drug rehabilitation program; the forming of a food cooperative; the establishment of volunteer committees where the skills of such craftspeople as carpenters, plumbers, lathers and engineers could be pooled for the use of other parishioners in times of need; consciousness raising sessions for women; programs in religion for retarded persons, as well as such traditional programs as A.A. and the newer but tremendously valuable Parent Effectiveness Training.[4] Once the goals for the year were established, and the objectives worked out with as much clarity and detail as possible, the parish personnel, perhaps in conjunction with the parish council, would prepare a State of the Parish address, delivered either at Mass or a special convocation, and published and mailed to every parishioner. The work of the year would then be the attempt to carry out the program, and the end of the year would bring a second published paper, or booklet, assessing and describing what had been done, and noting both strengths and weaknesses. This end of the year report could easily combine the next year's State of the Parish program, once it was established as a yearly (or two- or three-year) tradition.

---

4. See Thomas Gordon, *Parent Effectiveness Training*, New York: Peter Wyden, 1970.

One value of such a program is the conscious reflection it causes parishioners to bring to what they are doing, what needs to be done, and what can be done. A second value is the involvement of many parishioners who are not ordinarily a part of parish life. Another is that it provides a vehicle for accountability, as well as for publicity and sharing. As in the first draft of the National Catechetical Directory, space might be provided at the end of the document for parishioners to respond with additional suggestions. The document might include pictures, biographies of personnel, and a brief history of the parish as well.[5] Where the program has been tried, it has met with considerable success and admiration, and has served as a catalyst for surrounding parishes in their own religious lives.

QUESTION 4. *Does the parish seriously consider the option of stopping all formal education in religion for children?*
One alternative educational program considered by many parishes, especially those without parochial schools, is the planning of all educational activity around adults, with the benefit to children being an indirect kind of education, based on their participation in an adult community seriously involved with religious concerns. Instead of the child-teen-adult framework, parishes might consider a program for twenty to thirty year olds, one for thirty to forty-five year olds, one for forty-five to sixty-year olds, and one for those sixty and over. Just as children and youth have similar concerns due to developmental stages, so too do adults at each stage of adult life. The studies of Roger Gould of U.C.L.A., and Yale's Daniel Levinson and Harvard's George Vaillant have all, by now, been shared in the popular culture through *Time* and *New York* magazines,[6] and

---

5. See the brochure-pamphlet of St. Michael's-St. Edward's Parish in the Fort Greene section of Brooklyn, New York for an example of the power of a State of the Parish program.
6. See *Time*, April 28, 1975, "New Light on Adult Life Cycles," p. 69, and Gail Sheehy, "Catch-30 and other Predictable Crises of Growing Up Adult," in *New York*, November 17, 1973, pp. 30-51. See also Gail Sheehy, *Passages: Predictable Crises of Adult Life*, New York: E.P. Dutton, 1976.

these studies support the experience of adults as they move from young adulthood toward maturity. Ages 16-22 are generally seen as times of pulling up roots and leaving the family; 22-29 as a provisional adulthood or reaching out period where the task is the exploration of the possibilities for work, personal relationships and membership in society; 29 to 32 or 34 is seen almost universally as a time of crisis ("Catch-30" according to one writer),[7] where there is the dawning, difficult and painful presence of the fundamental question, "What *is* life all about?"; 35-43 is seen as the age of what is called the mid-life explosion, where the first emotional awareness of death comes with amazing force; 44-50 becomes a stage of restabilization, flowering, for men the discovery of their feminine sides and for women an acceptance of their masculinity; and after 50 comes the mellowing, the resting into life, and the first apprehensions of life's wholeness, acceptance, and peace. This research is of course only in a preliminary stage, but it is of significant assistance to any parish programmer who wishes to shift resources to the education of the adult community.

Along with studies such as these, there appears to be an even more potentially fruitful source for understanding the development of adult life in the work of James Fowler, research geared to the development of adult religious faith. To this time, Fowler has published little, but the reports of his work have been enormously helpful to any who have had contact with it. Of particular interest here, in speaking of the stages in the adult life cycle, are indications of what appear to be, in Fowler's tentative research, certain crises in the ongoing life process, which can help adults in their own understanding of their religious lives.[8] Fowler sketches, for example, the difference in one's understanding of religious formulations in one's own life, as the locus of authority shifts from one's parents, to dominant institutions, to one's peers, to oneself, toward a

---

7. Gail Sheehy, *ibid*.
8. James Fowler, "Toward a Developmental Perspective on Faith," *Religious Education*, Vol. LXIX, March-April 1974, pp. 207-219.

universal incorporation of all of these in some kind of integrated whole. Crises occur naturally because of a person's always expanding knowledge; a child may meet a crisis by dealing with fears of parent absence; an adult may meet a crisis by coming to grips with the terror of ambiguity. It would seem that a church community could be of enormous support to its members as they meet the individual and communal crises in religious faith coextensive with all of human life.

It is surprising that, when a parish decides to shift its resources to the adult community, the question almost always articulated is, "But what about the children?" The surprise comes from the fact that at present there is not the correlative concern "But what about the adults?" anywhere except at the rhetorical level, and in those few parishes that have decided to become adult communities into which children might grow. The crisis all adults go through where they are faced with the question "Shall I take this risk now, which may end in failure, or stay with the status quo, even though it has no meaning for me" is the question that all parishes now face with reference to adults depending on them as at least one source of religious development. Parishes may in fact be going through their own adult crisis. The question stands, however: Shall the parish continue the pattern of child-centeredness, or shall it take the risk of becoming a community of adult communities, bonded together by faith, hope, love and a vision of the future?

QUESTION 5. *Would the parish consider becoming a Religious Art Center for the diocese or vicariate?*

This question is directed to the suggestion that parishes might consider the novel alternative framework where all of the parish activity is artistic in form, execution and criteria. Just as there are some schools and summer camps where every activity is in some way tied to art, one parish in each diocese (it need not be a geographic parish) might be set up in such a way that its central focus was the relationship between the religious and the aesthetic, a relationship, it has already been remarked, which is quite natural and sympathetic.

In such a parish, the core of parish life could most certainly be the Eucharistic celebration, where all forms of art could be brought to bear on the liturgy. Groups could be responsible for design, graphics, sculpture and physical environment, where the best of contemporary and traditional art might be brought to execution; others could be involved with music, not only for the liturgy, but, besides that, where men and women might form a chorus under the direction of an expertly chosen and well paid director. Such a chorus would not be a church choir, but a chorale, where the objective would be the understanding, practice and performance of the finest sacred and secular music. Such a chorale could be a diocesan or regional resource for every kind of celebration, where the religious education would not be courses on doctrine but sessions where persons wishing to do so could approach the holy through the eight-part "Sanctus" of *Bach's Mass in B Minor*, to take but one example. How many parishioners, for example, might be involved in the experience of Easter and Christmas through learning and performing, in community with one another, the relevant portions of Handel's *Messiah*? Similar groups could also be formed with children and youth.

Dance could also be a vehicle for a parish using the aesthetic as a central concept in its educational program. This could take the form of sacred, interpretive dance as an expression during liturgy or prayer meetings; of dances as communal parish celebrations as they have traditionally occurred; of dances for young people in early teenage years where a young (read 'twentyish') combo could provide direction in group dancing that gets everyone, including the shyest, onto the floor without embarrassment. (I have witnessed youngsters learning to march to "When the Saints Go Marching In" under the guidance of a maestro little older than themselves and exulting in their adeptness in keeping up with the accelerating pace of the Alley Cat!) Finally, the very young can be instructed to "mess around with movement."

Lest this kind of experience be thought of as something superfluous or intended for those whose learning needs some frills, it must be insisted that what is being suggested here is an alternative framework where art is *the* mode for all of religious education, and not a "nice" extra which can be dispensed with as not really necessary for learning. Westerners are desperate for ways to be in touch with feeling, with loveliness, and with their own springs of creativity, and this is especially true, the less aesthetic one's surroundings.

"We had to find some means of bringing color and vitality into this grey world," Bess Bullough writes in recalling her experience in a primary school in a depressed mining town —"ways of making the school an exciting place where there was pride in achievement," as well as of making the children more sensitive to and aware of their environment. "We were eager to do anything that invited the children's involvement as feeling, thinking beings," she continues. "So we concentrated on physical education, drama, music and art."[9]

The only addition to this comment is that such "means of bringing color into individual lives" are as much needed by adults as by children.

Still another possibility for a Religious Art parish would be its use of drama. A presentation of "Fiddler on the Roof," for example, especially for those engaged in the execution of the performance, might teach far more about the pain involved in religious conviction than any cognitive course; a production of "The Roar of the Greasepaint—The Smell of the Crowd" or of "Gideon" more about the nature of dependence on God. Consider as an example, the following passage from Paddy Chayevsky's "Gideon":

The Messenger: O! Gideon, would you have your God a wandering magician, slapping a timbrel and kicking his heels?

Gideon: Do not rise in wrath against me, sir.

---

9. See Charles Silberman (ed.), *The Open Classroom Reader.* New York: Random House, 1973, p. 781.

The Messenger: I am not in wrath. I am plainly confused. And sore at heart. I have loved you and you have turned your back.

Gideon: I do find you personable, sir.

The Messenger: Personable! Gideon, one does not merely fancy God. I demand a splendid love from you, abandoned adoration, a torrent, a storm of love.

Gideon: (With almost unbearable kindness.) I'm afraid I'm not the splendid sort, my Lord. You want a less moderate man than I. I'm sure you shall find one soon enough, for you are an attractive God, and there are many men who will love you vigorously. I'm sure of that. (He offers his hand and smiles disarmingly.) Come, if I have given you some hurt, then clasp my hand and say that it is over with.

(The Messenger cannot help but be amused by this ingenuous fellow. He clasps Gideon's arm.)

The Messenger: I shall make you love me.

What attention to such a mode of learning might reveal to parishioners is the God who came and comes to them in time, who breaks into human history where they are, who approached and still approaches them in all the modes of being open to human beings: poetry, and song, and sorrow, and beauty, and, most of all, other people.

If the suggestion of an Aesthetic Parish seems too difficult to attempt, there is at least the possibility that a community within the parish could achieve something like this. Certainly, the DRE is in an ideal position to do something in this line, at the very least as the foundation for the formal education program. To those who panic at the thought, because they themselves have no artistic training or background, two observations are important. The first is that in every parish many persons with such gifts *do* exist, and might be called on for their assistance. The second is at a deeper level. Provision for the opportunity to tap one's aesthetic dimension is quite possibly in the realm of an *obligation* for a parish. For it is art which helps human beings, particularly as they come to the middle years of their lives, to come to grips with the human feeling our culture teaches them to hide so well, and without which they can never come to a fullness of appreciation for the beauty that is found in the divine.

QUESTION 6. *Have Open Education and the Open Classroom been seriously considered as alternative educational frameworks?*

Despite the fact that learning centers, open corridors, open classrooms and open education (the terms are often interchangeably used) are very much a part of general education, there seems little evidence as yet that parishes have chosen this approach as the basis of their own programs. The first reason may be an ignorance of the meaning of open education or open classroom.

Most simply, when open classrooms are referred to, they mean a facility, which may be a building, a room or a cluster of rooms, in which a wide variety of educational activities, sometimes called "learning centers," are available. The process of informal education (another synonym) has been developing in England since the end of World War II, but it is now growing rapidly as an alternative mode in the United States as well. Charles Silberman speaks of two fundamental issues underlying the shift to open education.

> I refer to a change in atmosphere—toward more humanness and understanding, toward more encouragement and trust. I also refer to a change in learning style—away from the teacher as the source of all knowledge, to the teacher as the facilitator of learning, away from the traditional whole-class orientation to more concern with individualized learn-

ing. These two changes, in atmosphere and in learning style, go hand in hand, for a focus on each individual learner can only occur if the classroom environment is transformed.[10]

The problem with introducing open education practices into church education is rarely the student; it is almost always problematical because those in teaching roles have not been exposed to learning in this kind of environment. For this reason, it would seem that the best place to introduce the concept of open education in a parish would be with those who form the teaching staff.[11]

Bove observed that usually teacher training programs conducted in parishes had a tendency to aim at meeting the needs of the inexperienced teachers, while those who were familiar with the content offered in introductory courses were often neglected. The type of learning situation she projected was therefore a learning lab aimed at providing teachers with continuing learning opportunities from self-instructional materials. These materials would be arranged in carrels, in a learning lab, according to subject areas, and the individual Coordinator would be responsible for designing individualized learning packages which might include several articles, a chapter from a book, the viewing of a filmstrip, an interview with the DRE on what had been learned, and the testing out of this learning and subsequent reflection, again with the DRE, on what had occurred, A sample package, available at the carrel, might be relevant copies of *PACE*, *The Living Light*, and *Religious Education*, each containing articles on parental involvement (if that were the subject area), a copy of Angela Barron McBride's *The Growth and Development of Mothers*,[12] a cassette from the Paulist *Come to the Father* Program, and directions on what to do with these materials. As received by the teacher initially, the packet would

---

10. *Ibid.*, pp. xvi-xvii.

11. For this and much of the subsequent material, I am indebted to a student of mine, Patricia Bove, who worked with this concept at Fordham. She taught me far more than I ever taught her.

12. New York: Harper and Row, 1973.

be found at one place, and at the beginning a set of directions
such as the following would be found:

> The following packet includes material which deals with
> parental involvement in the religious education of the
> child.
> 1. Read the article from *PACE* (pp. 227-236). List three
>   central ideas you received from this article.
> 2. Read the article from *The Living Light* (pp. 217-230).
>   What words, phrases, ideas struck you most? Write
>   these down now. Which ideas are you most anxious to
>   discuss further?
> 3. Read the article from *Religious Education* (pp. 98-
>   110). Does the reading of this article raise any new
>   questions for you?
> 4. Read chapter five of McBride's *Growth and Develop-
>   ment of Mothers*. Do you agree with McBride's ideas?
>   Have you ever experienced similar feelings?
> 5. Listen to the *Come to the Father* cassette. What new
>   questions does it raise for you?
> 6. Make an appointment with the Parish Coordinator to
>   reflect on the ideas you have gleaned, and to plan a
>   sharing session on them with other teachers.
> 7. Hold appointment; hold sharing session.
> 8. Evaluate sharing session; new ideas discovered in con-
>   versation with others; new insights; reinforcement of
>   previous learning.

Such is but one example of the kind of individualized packets that Coordinators might prepare. The work of preparation
is, of course, a huge one, but probably no greater than the
continual preparation of weekly teacher education sessions. The
positive advantages of a program like this is the advantage of
all open education. Learners select their own subject areas;
learners move at their own paces; materials are available in
many forms; opportunities for sharing are provided. For the
DRE, there is far more possibility for individual attention to
learners and a great cut-down on repetition.

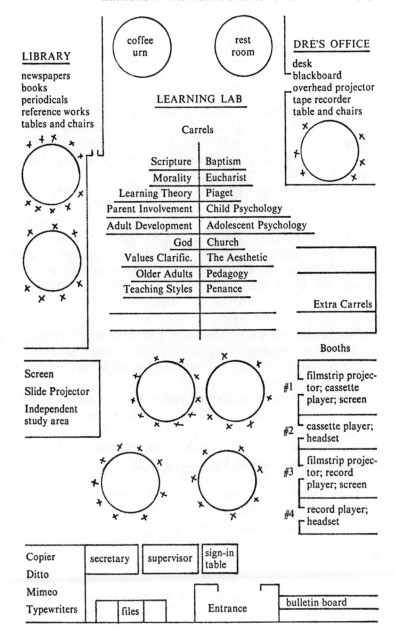

Another benefit of such a learning situation is its reliance on very little space. A rectory basement, an unused convent community room, a rented store, a large sacristy, or an empty classroom can be made to serve as learning center. Many designs are possible, but basically, the design of such a center could be similar to that shown here.[13] For the library and DRE's office, plywood walls could easily be constructed, office hours and learning lab hours could be established at the beginning of the year, and rotating secretaries, supervisors and librarians could assist in the lab management.

The major benefit of such a lab would not be solely for teachers, although they might be the ideal group with whom to start. Ideally, the lab could be open to all parishioners, and might lead to the establishment of several others. Where education of children continued to be a parish priority, the young people might be introduced to a process in their study of religion which many of them have already met in their regular school environments, an understanding of the richness and variety of religious learning could be encouraged, and an atmosphere of trust and freedom communicated. At the same time, whatever aspects of more formal educational practice have proven necessary and valuable for the learners in the past could be retained.

For Coordinators wishing to pursue this idea further, the literature on Open Education is vast. Silberman's work has already been noted. Other helpful volumes include Barbara Blitz' *The Open Classroom: Making It Work*, Boston: Allyn and Bacon, 1973, and Lillian Weber's *The English Infant School and Informal Education*, Englewood Cliffs, N.J.: Prentice Hall, 1971. However, the best understanding of Open Education can be gained by visiting open classrooms, talking to teachers and students engaged in them, and getting the feel of the procedures for oneself. Once that happens, it is time to open one's own Parish Learning Center.

---

13. Patricia Bove, "Learning Lab for Adult Religious Education," unpublished manuscript, New York: Fordham University, 1974, p. 5.

STRATEGY NO. 30: SUGGESTED PROGRAMS FOR OLDER ADULTS

Programs for senior citizens can be held on either a weekly or a monthly basis. Probably, beginning in September, the monthly is better as an initial possibility.

1. Initial Meeting: Introductions, basic questions, decisions on content.

2. Possible Themes: Changes in religion, church, Christianity

    Scripture

    Prayer

    Death and afterlife

    Cultural change

    Penance and reconciliation

    Sin and suffering

    Liturgical celebration

    Morality

3. Suggested Format: Rotation to the home of a different "host" or "hostess"; stress on simple preparations if any, i.e., coffee or tea and cookies—but no elaborate serving of food.

    Limit to one hour or one hour, fifteen minutes.

    Presence of a resource person to assist with materials, but not to be there to "run" the meeting, which should be done by the participants themselves.

    Liturgy or prayer service.

STRATEGY NO. 31: DESIGNING INDIVIDUALIZED LEARNING PACKETS

Below is a format which a DRE can use in designing Individualized Learning Packets for teachers and other learners. It is suggested that each packet have five or six sequential lessons, each following a format such as the one proposed.

ADULT LEARNING PACKET

LESSON ONE

A. Objectives:

1. You should be able to clarify what you mean by the term "adult."

2. You should become familiar with the stages of the life cycle as described by Erikson.

3. You should be able to give examples of various crises which occur in the adult life cycle.

B. Learning Activities:

1. Read *Design for Religion*, Chapter 6, "Adult Religious Education."

2. Read Erik Erikson, *Childhood and Society*, Chapter 7.

3. Read Malcolm Knowles, *The Adult Learner: A Neglected Species*, Chapter 3.

4. Listen to tape by William Glasser, *The Responsible World of Reality Therapy.*

C. Do:

1. Answer the following questions for yourself:
   (a) Upon reflection, who are two people you know to whom you spontaneously apply the word "adult"?
   (b) What are the qualities you associate with these persons which lead you to make this observation?
   (c) Can you identify any life conditions which seem to lead to a person's becoming adult?
   (d) Can you identify any ways in which you see adulthood reflected in the religious area of life?

2. Interview three other people, asking the same questions.

3. Spend a half hour in reflection and prayer on what you have discovered thus far.

D. Summarize what you have learned.

Coordinators now fill in the following pages according to a similar format, choosing either this topic or one more needed in their own situations. It is quite possible that you will find yourself adapting material you have previously presented as you devise these packets. Experienced teachers might be responsible for preparing packets as well.

STRATEGY NO. 32

LESSON TWO

A. Objectives:

B. Learning Activities:

Read:

Listen to: (tape)

View: (film or filmstrip)

Other:

C. Do: (Personal activity based on the above. This may be interviews, discussions, teaching a class, having a conference with the DRE, conducting further research, etc.)

D. Summarize: Some activity designed to integrate the above.

STRATEGY NO. 33

LESSON THREE

A. Objectives:

B. Learning Activities:

C. Do:

D. Summarize:

STRATEGY NO. 34

LESSON FOUR

A. Objectives:

B. Learning Activities:

C. Do:

D. Summarize:

STRATEGY NO. 35

LESSON FIVE

A. Objectives:

B. Learning Activities:

C. Do:

D. Summarize:

STRATEGY NO. 36

LESSON SIX

A. Objectives:

B. Learning Activities:

C. Do:

D. Summarize:

10
Coordinators: Religious Resource

Coordinators are a special brand of person. Anyone who has read the preceding pages has some sense of the energy, determination, patience and sheer perseverance needed for the multi-tasked position that is theirs. The specialness I would associate with them, however, is of another kind. I refer to a certain quality of personhood observable in most Coordinators throughout the country, whether they are men, women, short, tall, members of religious orders, married or single.

The quality is best summarized as a relaxation *with* and *into* the position that is theirs, an ability not to get too flustered, too excited or too distressed when things do not go exactly as planned. Perhaps the best image to describe this quality is that of the Chocolate Soldier. Once upon a time, in battles, new recruits and freshly commissioned officers would appear on the battle lines, clean and starched, with swords gleaming, shoes and buttons polished, and every hair brushed and plastered into place. Not so the veteran soldiers who had been around for some time and were in for the long haul. Passing inspection was not a particular priority for them, especially on such superficial criteria as appearance, nor did they find it important always to be ready for confrontation. What *was* important, however, was that they had time for human companionship, that they were nourished, and that they had time for a little joy. So, they tended to fill their pockets, not with bullets, but with chocolates. During a long, hard battle, it was a great comfort to reach into one's pocket and pull out a piece of candy. Hence the name, and the image: Chocolate Soldier.

With the greatest respect, reverence and affection, I should like to suggest that Coordinators are Chocolate Soldiers. From New England to San Francisco, from Michigan to Mississippi, I have met hundreds of them, and it is my observation that they are not only doing a fantastic job; they are also the most important people in the U.S. church today and the ones most responsible for changing it fundamentally. In saying this, I hope I am not letting out a secret; Coordinators have, up to now, been able to keep a very low profile, and the revolution has been a gentle, quiet and non-violent one, but it is a revolution, and perhaps the time has come to recognize it. Coordinators are changing, and already have changed the face of the church in this country, and there is no reason to think they will not continue to do so.

Two major reasons stand out in my mind for calling the presence and efforts of Coordinators a revolution. The first is the quality of their presence to the people in their parishes. The job description of the Coordinator generally speaks of him or her as a religious resource person, and it is this description I should like to address first. All of the duties mentioned throughout this book, concerned with the selection of materials, familiarity with theological trends, and the ability to reflect theologically with the community, are included here; but at a deeper level the Coordinator's presence as a person concerned with the religious quality of other lives is what strikes the observer most forcibly. Coordinators tend to be persons with a good deal of age and experience who listen well and treat other people with care. The aspect of care is another quality observable in the Coordinator, and it is a particularly religious characteristic. Care, it is said, was walking along the river one day, picking up earth and thinking, "Wouldn't it be wonderful if there could be human beings?" But because Care couldn't *make* human beings, didn't have that power, Care asked God to take the earth and breathe life into it. And God did. What happened after that was that it was decided that since God had breathed life into human beings, God would receive them when they died; God was where they were going. Because they were made from the earth, from the *humus*, they would be called human. But because Care had thought of them in the first place, God said that Care would possess them all their lives.[1]

In U.S. parishes today, Care finds preeminent embodiment in the DRE. Countless individual persons have, through their contacts with Coordinators, been able to treat, in the freeing atmosphere DRE's tend to set up, the issues of life and death that eat at their insides—the failing marriage, the son or daughter on drugs, the crippling economic bind, the terror and guilt that accompany sacramental reception under circumstances poorly understood or the non-communion for no reason, the loneliness of old age. The Coordinator stands in the parish as someone who cares, who is there, who listens, and who assists people to reflect on their lives, not only with the systematic answers of theology, but with the piety and reverence drawn from a gospel that says: "Look at the birds of the air; they do not sow or reap or gather into barns, yet your heavenly Father feeds them. Are not you of much more value than they?" The revolutionary quality of this attitude is that it is creating a broader, deeper and more illuminated understanding of religion than has been present in the past. It is breaking down a narrow, provincial vision, and bringing to birth one that looks outward toward all people and all creation as sacraments of the Holy.

In no way is this affirmation of the DRE intended to depreciate those clergy in parishes who have always fulfilled this kind of role, and who continue to do so today. The change, however, is that there is now an additional person, or persons, fulfilling the same role, and, more often than not, this person is a woman, a major change, and/or a non-ordained person, which tends to mitigate the problems sometimes encountered by those whose training and background causes them, unfortunately, to see priests as authority or father figures.

What I am trying to point to here is that the DRE, as a religious resource person, may professionally possess theologi-

---

1. For bringing my attention to this myth, which she discovered in Heidegger's *Being and Time*, I am indebted to Elinor Stetson of Boston College.

cal background and insight which supports his or her activity, but that that activity itself is a religious kind of activity, a healing, reconciling and sacramental relating to other human beings. The Coordinator deals with the substance of theology cognitively, in formal courses and teacher education situations; informally, the DRE's theology is expressed in the way she or he relates to the people with whom he or she comes in contact. There are two major results of this activity. One is that even if it is not articulated, the relationship between theology and the religious qualities of human life tend to be seen as mutual and complementary. The second is that the Coordinator's presence as a religious man or religious woman tends to catalyze others in the community to live out their own religious attitudes toward one another in a similar way. Thus the Coordinator is, indeed, a religious resource: someone who can be turned to for support or help; an available supply that can be drawn upon when needed; someone to be used to a community's advantage. However, she or he is a resource in an even more profound sense. A *source* is a place or thing from which something comes or derives, a point of origin. Even more significantly, a source is one who causes, creates or initiates something. It is this second sense that is most important today. The Coordinator is re-causing, re-creating, re-initiating, and what is being re-created and re-initiated is a new understanding of religious ministry.

It is curious to note that ten years ago no one in the Roman Catholic Church except the clergy spoke of his work as ministry. The use of this term in the wider church is quite recent, 1969 or 1970, which was about the same time that Coordinators were beginning to appear on the scene in large numbers. The term, as it is used, appears to have four separate meanings, all of which overlap in one way or another. The first use occurs when speaking of one's profession, particularly if it is a helping profession, as one's ministry. Thus the affirmation: "My ministry is health care," or "education," or "social work," or "counseling." This rendering of the term can have both positive and negative meanings. Negatively, it can be a subtle put-down of other professionals engaged in the same field who are not related to the church, especially if one says, "When you are in ministry, you do *more* than the ordinary educator." I would suspect that any genuine educator is as humanly concerned with the caring elements of her or his work as it is possible to be, and would quite rightly not take too kindly the affirmation that it is only a job, when it is not. George Dennison[2] and Jonathan Kozol,[3] to take but two examples, could not have been more concerned with the lives of their students than they were. Positively, of course, all the professions might be thought of as human ministries, and the person claiming ministry as the description of his or her work would have to acknowledge that all in the helping professions are engaged in ministry. The concern, care and loving attitudes connoted by the term are obviously, then, not owned by church people.

A second use of the term ministry is in religious orders of men and women. Again, seven or eight years ago, no Provincial Chapter had a committee on ministry. There was one on the apostolate, but the term apostolate appears to have given way to ministry, and the meaning here becomes similar to the one alluded to above where one's work is one's ministry. The only distinction is that some orders will claim the reason for their existence is ministry, and the distinguishing mark of a religious order is that it is a group of people whose lives are engaged in a particular ministry in the church. On the one hand, this may be true as far as it goes, although most religious orders today have members in a variety of works. But if it is given as the raison d'être for the existence of the religious orders, it still raises identity questions for the order in a changing culture. Many other institutions in our society, not affiliated with the church, engage in the same kind of work as religious orders. Thus it is at least problematical to claim that the reason the order exists is to do ministry. If, however, a religious order exists to demonstrate an alternative kind of community, this may indeed be a ministry, but once again the question arises why this word is the one chosen to define the life style.

---

2. See *The Lives of Children*, New York: Vintage Books, 1969.
3. See *Death at an Early Age*, Boston: Houghton-Mifflin Company, 1967.

The third and fourth uses of ministry, particularly by Coordinators, come when one asks them directly, "What *do* you
mean when you say your work is ministry?" The first response
tends to be the giving of an example of a helping activity, such
as visiting people who have had a recent death in the family,
driving someone to the dentist, calling a shut-in—the kinds of
activities that have always been spoken of in the church as the
spiritual and corporal works of mercy. It is quite true that
DRE's spend a great deal of time carrying out these activities,
but again, obviously, these are works demanded from all in the
church. What this response gets at is the notion that, if such
works are ministry, then all in the church are involved in ministry, and the scriptural affirmation that there is one priesthood
but many ministries is quite accurate.

This leads to the fourth and most fundamental understanding of ministry that is emerging today. Plainly and simply,
ministry is the doing of that work formerly allowed only to the
ordained: ministry is priestly activity. The change is of enormous significance. In the first place, ministry is seen more
as a work in a community, priestly work, which if one
looks closely raises the issue that a priest is not something one
becomes, but that priestliness is an *activity* that is called for by
a community.

Realistically, this would and could be leading to a church
where the qualities determining one's role as priestly would be
quite different from what they are today, but more similar to
what they were in earlier times when one was recognized as
being priestly and raised up by the people to perform priestly
functions. Although there would be sociological and historical
barriers, there would be no lasting reasons why those holding a
priestly office in a community might not be elected, or emerge,
or be appointed for a period of time to be determined mutually,
and there would certainly be no solid reasons (as there are few if
any now) why both women and men, married and single, could
not fulfill this role, as they are quietly doing today without fuss,
publicity, or, it must be added, ecclesiastical approval.

The remaining question to be answered would be this last